DATE DUE

JE 6'98			
JY 21'99			

DEMCO 38-296

A Student's Guide to JAPANESE AMERICAN Genealogy

Oryx American Family Tree Series

A Student's Guide to JAPANESE AMERICAN Genealogy

By Yoji Yamaguchi

 Oryx Press
1996

Copyright 1996 by The Rosen Publishing Group, Inc.
Published in 1996 by The Oryx Press

¹l Road

ublication may be reproduced
ʼ means, electronic or mechan-
ng, or by any information
permission in writing

Printed and bound in the United States of America

∞ The paper used in this publication meets the minimum
requirements of American National Standard for Information
Science—Permanence of Paper for Printed Library Materials,
ANSI Z39.48, 1984.

Library of Congress Cataloging-in-Publication Data
Yamaguchi, Yoji.
    A student's guide to Japanese American genealogy / Yoji Yamaguchi.
        p.   cm.—(Oryx American family tree series)
    Includes bibliographical references and index.
    ISBN 0-89774-979-0
    1. Japanese Americans—Genealogy—Handbooks, manuals,
etc. I. Title. II. Series.
E184.J3Y335   1996
929'.1'089956073—dc20   95-36130
                                                            CIP

Contents

Introduction

Who Makes History?

We commonly think of history as a drama played out by a handful of famous people. Although it may affect our own lives, the assumption goes, we are powerless to affect it. We can only watch like spectators in the stands.

In textbooks, historical events are described as the result of abstract and unseen forces driving nation-states, kingdoms, factions, and mass movements. The Declaration of Independence, the Emancipation Proclamation, the New Deal—these are some of the milestones of this country's history. Yet in between are the stories of millions of people who lived through and took part in the crucial moments of history. Their names and faces have largely been forgotten.

Conventional history must necessarily generalize. But generalizations about people are of limited usefulness. Some families lives' may seem like "textbook examples," whereas others do not fit any commonplace idea. Students read textbooks, hear lectures, watch documentaries, memorize famous names, dates, and places. All the while troves of information are in attics and basements, in scrapbooks and albums, on walls and refrigerator doors. Every family has had a part in this country's history.

In his classic novel *War and Peace*, the Russian novelist Leo Tolstoy depicts the French and Austrian invasions of Russia from 1805 to 1812. But the main characters of his story are not the famous generals or politicians but the Rostovs, a landowning family. Their private dramas—the quarrels, struggles, triumphs, hopes, and fears—and those of millions of others like them, in Tolstoy's view, make up the sum of history.

1

Why Study Japanese American Genealogy?

Japanese Americans have been called the "model minority": Since the first immigrants toiled in the cane fields of Hawaii in the late nineteenth century, Japanese Americans have enjoyed enormous success professionally and socially. Japanese Americans comprise only 1 percent of the country's population. But they have excelled in a wide variety of fields, from government leaders such as Hawaii's Senator Daniel K. Inouye to athletes such as 1992 Olympic gold medalist Kristi Yamaguchi.

But the story of Japanese Americans has not always been an easy one. The first generation of Japanese immigrants, or *issei*, endured severe hardships and made enormous sacrifices of body and soul. And it was only roughly fifty years ago, during World War II, that Japanese Americans were perhaps the most hated group in all America, for events that were beyond their control.

If you are a Japanese American student, exploring your family's past is exploring your own past. The experiences of your ancestors are part of a narrative that has culminated in you. Their lives, for better or worse, have shaped yours. In the process of learning who your ancestors were, you may be surprised to discover just who you are.

Even if you are not Japanese American, the story of Japanese Americans is an important part of this country's heritage. As the poet Walt Whitman wrote, America "is not a nation but a Nation of nations." President John F. Kennedy (a second-generation Irish American) noted that ours is "a society of immigrants, each of whom had begun life anew on an equal footing. This was the secret of America: a nation of peoples with a fresh memory of old traditions who dared to explore new frontiers."

In genealogy, or family history, among the most important tools are people's memories. As one goes further back in time, written records, photos, and artifacts may become harder to find. Much useful information is not recorded anywhere. It exists solely in memory.

Your genealogical research may lead you to information about Japanese history and culture. Modernization in late-nineteenth-century Japan resulted in the abolition of the *samurai,* Japan's ancient warrior class. Unaccustomed to their new lives of poverty and lack of status, some *samurai* banded together in revolts against the government.

But memories are not permanent. They fade with age and die with the people who hold them—unless they are passed along. Just as species of animals, once extinct, are gone forever, so too are memories. Once forgotten, people, places, and events are lost forever.

A story is told about the Greek philosopher Aristotle: One day he meets a carpenter who shows him a beautiful old knife. The carpenter explains that the knife has belonged to his family for many generations and adds: "We have had to change the handle a few times and the blade a few times, but otherwise it is the same knife."[1]

The knife, of course, has changed: The original parts that composed it no longer exist. But to the carpenter it is the same knife his ancestors used. Memories work in a similar fashion. When we hear the life stories of ancestors, those stories become our memories even though the original person or event may be long past. Your search through the past is an experience you can share with others. The memories of those who came before us can live on.

About This Book

This book is a guide to the study of genealogy, or family history, through the use of historical documents, artifacts, and private records. While it is mainly intended for people who wish to trace their family roots, it can also be used by anyone interested in the lives of Japanese Americans throughout the years. Some of the following chapters describe how to find records that are publicly available.

When you research your genealogy, you will not only learn about your ancestors' birth and death dates but also about Japanese emigrants' collective history and culture in Japan, how that changed or stayed the same when they immigrated and settled in the United States, and the motivating factors that caused these changes. Part of genealogical research is to find out how history individually influenced your own

---

[1] Adapted from A. K. Ramanujan, *Folktales from India* (New York: Pantheon, 1992), p. xx.

forebears, and in one way or another this history affected all our ancestors.

If you are tracing not your own family's past, but someone else's, always be respectful of other people's feelings. Never look up the records of living persons without their permission. Even if you are researching someone who died many years ago, remember that he or she may have descendants living somewhere, maybe in your own neighborhood. Never use your research in a way that might cause other people pain or public embarrassment. This is not only disrespectful; it could be illegal. Every person has a legal right to privacy, and the laws protecting that right are complicated. Thus you would do best to stick to families whose members will not only permit your search, but welcome it and help it along.

After all, much of your search will depend on memories, which can be tapped only by asking people. A stranger who has no personal connection with you might not want to discuss his or her family with you. If someone objects to your research, do not proceed. Instead, you can explore other areas of Japanese American history. What follows is a brief account of that history.

Resources

STARTING YOUR EXPLORATION

Avakian, Monique. *The Meiji Restoration and the Rise of Modern Japan.* **Columbus, OH: Silver Burdett Press, 1991.**

> A concise but in-depth look at the events leading up to the modern Japanese state. Includes photographs, maps, and diagrams.

Beller, Susan P. *Roots for Kids: Genealogy Anyone Can Understand.* **Crozet, VA: Betterway, 1989.**

> A guide to genealogical research written primarily for children.

Hirabayashi, L. *Discrimination: Japanese Americans Struggle for Equality.* **Vero Beach, FL: Rourke Publishing Group, 1992.**

> A historical perspective on discrimination faced by Japanese Americans. Discusses the more recent revival of anti-Japanese sentiment caused by fears of Japan's economic superiority.

Kawaguchi, Gary. *Tracing Our Japanese Roots.* **Santa Fe: John Muir Publications, 1995.**

> Written primarily for young children, a concise account of Japanese American history and culture.

Kitano, Harry. *The Japanese Americans.* **Introduction by Senator Daniel Patrick Moynihan. New York: Chelsea House, 1988.**

A short, basic introduction to the history of Japanese Americans.

Kogawa, Joy. *Naomi's Road.* **New York: Oxford University Press, 1988.**

A children's novel about the Nakane family, a Japanese Canadian family sent to an internment camp in British Columbia during World War II.

Rolater, F. S. *Japanese Americans.* **Vero Beach, FL: Rourke Publishing Group, 1992.**

Part of an American Voices series, this book traces the history of Japanese Americans, explaining why and where they settled in the United States.

Takaki, Ronald. *Issei and Nisei: The Settling of Japanese America.* **New York: Chelsea House, 1995.**

Oral histories, immigrants' writings, and examples from the author's family are used to describe the experiences of Japanese Americans. Black-and-white photos illustrate the text.

Uchida, Yoshiko. *The Invisible Thread.* **Columbus, OH: Silver Burdett Press, 1991.**

A memoir about the author's childhood and adolescence in the 1930s and '40s.

———. *Samurai of Gold Hill.* **New York: Scribner's, 1972.**

A children's novel set in 1869 about the ill-fated Wakamatsu colony in California, the first Japanese American community in the mainland United States.

———. *Journey to Topaz.* **New York: Creative Arts, 1985.**

The story of eleven-year-old Yuki Sakane and her family when they are forced to leave their California home during the relocation and internment of Japanese Americans during World War II.

————. *Journey Home*. New York: Macmillan, 1992.

A sequel to *Journey to Topaz*, set in the years after the war. It tells of the hardships and hostility the Sakane family encounter when they try to return to their home.

Westridge Young Writers Workshop. *Kids Explore America's Japanese American Heritage*. **Santa Fe: John Muir Publications, 1994.**

Students write about Japanese American culture and history, covering topics such as food and festivals, martial arts, poetry, and the experiences of Japanese Americans in internment camps.

NONFICTION—GENERAL

Adamic, Louis. *From Many Lands*. **New York: Harper & Brothers, 1939.**

Personal accounts of immigrants of various ethnicities. Narratives of the immigrants' home countries and of their experiences in the United States meld to form a positive portrait of the immigrant experience at a time when immigration was not held in high esteem.

Bennett, Archibald F. *Finding Your Forefathers in America*. **Salt Lake City: Bookcraft Co., 1957.**

Regional and ethnic guide to genealogical research in the United States. Includes chapters about general research methods, accessing libraries and archives, and producing pedigrees. Historical information specific to genealogy includes land records, Bible records, birth and death records, and letters.

Bromwell, William J. *History of Immigration to the United States*. **New York: Augustus M. Kelley Publishers, 1969.**

Reprint of original 1855 edition lists statistics about immigrants who arrived between 1819 and 1855. No individuals are named, but lists give statistics about the numbers who immigrated, from which countries, and their occupations by port of entry. Indexed by calendar year. Includes synopsis of immigration and naturalization laws.

Chan, Sucheng. *Asian Americans: An Interpretive History.* **Boston: Twayne Publishers, 1991.**

Twayne's Immigrant Heritage of America Series. A general history of Asian Americans. The book details reasons for immigration, discrimination that Asian immigrants have faced, and the formation of Asian American communities.

Demos, John. *Past, Present, and Personal: The Family and the Life Course in American History.* **New York: Oxford University Press, 1986.**

Eight essays covering the entire span of American history, discussing such topics as the changing role of fatherhood throughout history. Some of the essays are difficult reading.

Dublin, Thomas, ed. *Immigrant Voices: New Lives in America, 1773–1986.* **Urbana: University of Illinois Press, 1993.**

First-person accounts of the immigrant experience for Asian, European, and Mexican families, covering 200 years.

Fairchild, Henry Pratt. *Immigration: A World Movement and Its American Significance.* **New York: Macmillan, 1913.**

History of immigration, its causes and effects, conditions of immigrants including exploitation, crime, and standards of living. Contains a bibliography.

Gordon, Michael, ed. *The American Family in Social-Historical Perspective.* **New York: St. Martin's Press, 1973.**

A collection of essays on American family history.

Harriss, John, ed. *The Family: A Social History of the*

Twentieth Century. **New York: Oxford University Press, 1991.**

A general account of the relationship between private life and the landmark events of this century. It also examines the changing patterns of family life, such as societies' attitudes toward the young and old.

Kessner, Thomas, and Caroli, Betty Boyd. *Today's Immigrants, Their Stories: A Look at the Newest American.* **New York: Oxford University Press, 1982.**

Discussion of the Immigration Act of 1965 and its effect in changing immigration. Personal stories by immigrants after 1965.

Kingston, Maxine Hong. *Chinamen.* **New York: Vintage, 1989.**

A semifictional account of the author's immigrant ancestors and their early experiences in America.

Levine, Daniel B.; Hill, Kenneth; and Warren, Robert, eds. *Immigration Statistics: A Story of Neglect.* **Washington, DC: National Academy Press, 1985.**

Discussion of the history of immigration policy in the United States, the need for statistics on immigration, the Immigration and Naturalization Service, and the problems of data gathering and analysis.

Mooney, Peter J. *The Impact of Immigration on the Growth and Development of the U.S. Economy, 1890–1920.* **New York: Garland Publishing, 1990.**

History of the contributions of immigrants to the U.S. economy and industry. Includes discussion of agricultural labor, the formation of capital, and wage structures.

Panunzio, Constantine. *Immigration Crossroads.* **New York: Macmillan, 1927.**

Analysis of the immigration problem and the legislative debate surrounding it.

Roucek, J. S. *The Immigrant in Fiction and Biography.* **New York: Bureau for Intercultural Education, 1945.**

A bibliography of fictional and biographical works about immigrants from Japan, China, Syria, and most European countries.

Russo, David J. *Families and Communities: A New View of American History.* **Nashville, TN: American Association for State and Local History, 1974.**

This book proposes revising American history through a focus on family and local history.

Seller, Maxine. *To Seek America.* **Englewood, NJ: Jerome S. Ozer, 1977.**

Discussion of ethnicity, ethnic communities, and their institutions and press and the role of these in immigrants' lives in America. Includes chapters about urban ghettos, settling the frontier, building ethnic communities, the change in attitude toward ethnic groups, and immigration after 1924.

Shoumatoff, Alex. *A Mountain of Names: A History of the Human Family.* **New York: Vintage, 1990.**

A history of kinship and ancestry in cultures throughout the world. Includes a discussion of Japanese naming practices.

Watts, Jim, and Davis, Allen F. *Generations: Your Family in Modern American History.* **New York: McGraw-Hill, 1988.**

A collection of essays combining personal accounts and general history.

Weitzman, David. *Underfoot: An Everyday Guide to Exploring the American Past.* **New York: Scribner's, 1976.**

A useful guide for beginners researching local and regional histories.

Wheeler, Thomas C., ed. *The Immigrant Experience: The Anguish of Becoming American.* **Baltimore: Penguin Books, 1972.**

A compendium of anecdotal accounts by persons of various ethnicity about the immigrant experience with particular focus on alienation and the loss of ethnic identity.

Winslow, Donald J. *Life-Writing: A Glossary of Terms in Biography, Autobiography, and Related Forms,* **2d ed. Honolulu: University of Hawaii Press, 1995.**

A reference guide to the terms involved in the study of genealogy, biography, and autobiography, containing three hundred entries.

Wright, Norman E. *Preserving Your American Heritage.* **Provo, UT: Brigham Young University Press, 1981.**

A guide to conducting a genealogical search, including a list of sources, with emphasis on the diversity of the country's heritage.

JAPANESE AMERICAN FAMILIES

Hoobler, Dorothy, and Hoobler, Thomas. *The Japanese American Family Album.* **New York: Oxford University Press, 1995.**

Using diaries, letters, interviews, photos, newspaper and magazine articles, oral histories, and profiles of famous figures, this "family album" documents the experiences of Japanese American immigrants.

Kessler, Lauren. *Stubborn Twig: Three Generations in the Life of a Japanese American Family.* **New York: Random House, 1994.**

A chronicle of the Yasui family and their experiences spanning the entire century.

Kitano, Harry. *Japanese Americans: The Evolution of*

a Subculture. **Englewood Cliffs, NJ: Prentice-Hall, 1976.**

A more comprehensive study of Japanese Americans.

Kitano, Harry, and Kikumura, Akemi. "The Japanese American Family" in *Ethnic Families in America: Patterns and Variations*. Edited by Charles H. Minel and Robert W. Habenstein. New York: Elsevier, 1976.

A study of relationships and interactions in Japanese American families.

Nakano, Mei. *Japanese American Women: Three Generations, 1890–1990*. Sebastopol, CA: Mina Press, 1990.

A study of three generations of Japanese American women, their roles and accomplishments. Includes Grace Shibata's extended remembrance of her mother, "Okaasan."

Yanagisako, Sylvia Junko. *Transforming the Past: Tradition and Kinship Among Japanese Americans*. Stanford, CA: Stanford University Press, 1985.

A study of Japanese American kinship, focusing on marriage, parent-children relationships, and relationships between brothers and sisters.

FICTION ABOUT JAPANESE AMERICANS

Kadohata, Cynthia. *The Floating World: A Novel*. New York: Viking, 1989.

The story of three generations of a Japanese American family living in the same household.

Shigekuni, Julie. *A Bridge Between Us*. New York: Anchor Books, 1995.

The story of four generations of women in a Japanese American family in San Francisco.

Watanabe, Sylvia. *Talking to the Dead: Stories.*
New York: Doubleday, 1992.

A collection of ten stories about Japanese Americans in present-day Hawaii.

ANTHOLOGIES

Asian Women United of California, eds. *Making Waves: An Anthology of Writings By and About Asian American Women.* Boston: Beacon Press, 1989.

A collection of fiction, nonfiction, poetry, and memoirs about politics, history, culture, sexuality, and other issues.

Brown, Wesley, and Ling, Amy, eds. *Imagining America: Stories from the Promised Land.* New York: Persea Books, 1991.

A collection of fiction by and about immigrant Americans.

————. *Personal Narratives from the Promised Land.* New York: Persea Books, 1992.

A companion to the above title, this volume collects non-fiction accounts and essays by immigrant Americans.

Bruhac, Carol, and Watanabe, Sylvia, eds. *Home to Stay: Asian American Women's Fiction.* Greenfield Center, NY: The Greenfield Review Press, 1990.

A collection of stories by Asian American women.

Bruhac, Joseph, ed. *Breaking Silence: An Anthology of Contemporary Asian American Poets.* Greenfield Center, NY: The Greenfield Review Press, 1983.

A collection of poetry by Asian American writers.

Chin, Jeffery Paul; Chin, Frank, et al, eds. *Aiiieeeee! An Anthology of Asian American Writers.* Washington, DC: Howard University Press, 1974.

A collection of fiction, nonfiction, poetry, and drama by Asian Americans.

————. *The Big Aiiieeeee! An Anthology of Chinese American and Japanese American Fiction.* New York: Meridian, 1991.

> This volume features fiction, nonfiction, poetry, and drama by Chinese American and Japanese American writers.

Hagedorn, Jessica, ed. *Charlie Chan Is Dead: An Anthology of Contemporary Asian American Literature.* New York: Penguin, 1993.

> A collection of fifty stories by Asian American writers.

The Hawk's Well: A Collection of Japanese American Art and Literature. San Jose, CA: Asian American Art Projects, 1986.

> Contains art and literature from Japanese American artists and writers.

Hong, Maria, ed. *Growing Up Asian American: An Anthology.* New York: William Morrow, 1993.

> Thirty-two Asian American writers, from the nineteenth century to the 1990s, write short stories and essays about childhood.

Hongo, Garrett, ed. *The Open Boat: Poems from Asian America.* New York: Anchor, 1993.

> A collection of poetry by thirty-one Asian American poets.

————. *Under Western Eyes: Personal Essays from Asian America.* New York: Anchor, 1995.

> Literary, political, and personal, this anthology of autobiographical writing by Asian American writers examines the question of identity.

Kitano, Harry H. L. *Japanese Americans: The Evolution of a Subculture.* Englewood Cliffs, NJ: Prentice-Hall, 1969.

The culture of Japanese Americans is surveyed by a prominent Japanese American scholar.

Mirikitani, Janice, et al., eds. *Ayumi: A Japanese American Anthology.* **San Francisco: Japanese American Anthology Committee, 1980.**

An anthology of Japanese American literature by various authors.

Chapter 1
History

The Meiji Restoration

When a fleet of United States naval ships commanded by
Commodore Matthew C. Perry sailed into Edo (now Tokyo)
harbor in July 1853, Japan was a closed nation. Foreign
ships were banned from its ports, and travel abroad was
forbidden. Since 1638, the country had been ruled by a
succession of warlords of the Tokugawa family.

Backed by his powerful warships, Perry pressured the
Japanese to open their shores. On March 31, 1854, the
Treaty of Kanagawa was signed, allowing American ships to
enter two Japanese ports.

This capitulation to American demands made the
Tokugawa government look weak, and in 1868 it was forced
from power. The emperor Mutsuhito formed a parliamentary government with a new constitution. Thus began the
period known as the Meiji (Enlightened) era, or the Meiji
Restoration.

After 1868, Japan rushed to modernize itself by introduc-
ing Western institutions and technology. A modern navy was
built, modeled after England's. The cabinet was based on
the German example. The public education system followed
that of the United States. Engineers from the Netherlands
and France worked on the country's infrastructure.

These rapid changes caused tremendous social and economic upheaval. To pay for its reforms, the government
levied stiff land taxes on farmers. But the average farm in
Japan was of less than three acres and produced scarcely
enough to feed a family. Roughly 300,000 farmers lost
their lands. During the 1880s, Japan's agricultural
economy underwent a severe depression. In the poorer

rural districts some people were reduced to eating wheat chaff and grass.

Farmers were not the only ones who suffered. To build its new army, the government started a national draft. The *samurai* class was abolished and the private armies of the nobility were disbanded. Accustomed to lives of prestige and security, *samurai* suddenly found themselves living on meager pensions. Many were reduced to poverty; others resorted to armed revolt. The most infamous incident took place in 1877 at Satsuma, where former *samurai* laid siege to an army garrison but were defeated by government troops.

While the country was reforming itself, scholars and emissaries were traveling and bringing back accounts of life in the West. One of the more famous of these was Fukuzawa Yukichi, who exhorted the Japanese to study abroad for the good of the country. Japanese were seeing a world elsewhere. The Meiji government's restrictions on mass emigration began to loosen.

Early Pioneers

Japanese immigration to the United States did not begin until the 1890s, but as early as the thirteenth century Japanese fishing boats were sometimes caught in the *Kuroshio* (Black Current) and swept to the Hawaiian islands. In 1841 a sailor named Manjiro was shipwrecked in Hawaii and later educated in the United States, where he changed his name to John Mung. He later returned to Japan to speak publicly about his life in America.

In the first year of the Meiji era, or "Meiji One," Hawaiian plantation owners conducted an experiment. A group of 150 Japanese laborers were recruited from Yokohama, a port city, to work on Hawaii's plantations. But these *gannenmono* ("first-year men") were mostly city dwellers who had never seen a farm before. They were ill-suited to farmwork and resented the harsh treatment of their Hawaiian bosses, so they refused to work. When the Japanese government heard of their situation, it ordered them home. Only fifty of the original men returned to Japan; the rest stayed.

The decline of the traditional *samurai* class and the increasing European influence on Japan is evident in this portrait of two *samurai* in 1868, who carry Japanese weapons but wear European clothing.

The first Japanese immigrants to the mainland United States arrived in San Francisco on May 27, 1869. A small group of former *samurai*, farmers, and merchants settled on a 600-acre farm in Gold Hill, California, and called themselves the Wakamatsu Tea and Silk Farm Colony. They planted mulberry trees for silk farming, bamboo shoots, tea seeds, grape seedlings, and other native Japanese plants. But the plants could not adapt to the California soil. Within two years, the colony disbanded.

The First Waves

On February 8, 1885, 943 Japanese immigrants (676 men, 159 women, and 108 children) aboard the ship *City of Tokio* arrived in Honolulu, followed on June 17 of that year by another 939 men, 35 women, and 14 children. The adults were hired as laborers to work in Hawaii's fields and factories. Fieldhands worked ten hours a day, six days a week; factory workers worked twelve hours. The men were paid $9 a month (plus a $6 food allowance); the women were paid $6 a month (plus $4 for food).

These were the first of 29,000 Japanese to immigrate to Hawaii under a treaty signed between Hawaii and Japan in 1886. (Hawaii did not become a U.S. territory until 1898.) From 1886 to 1894, the Japanese government sponsored workers immigrating to Hawaii. By the end of the nineteenth century, 65,000 Japanese had immigrated to Hawaii.

The farm depression, plus demand for cheap labor from the United States, compelled Japan to permit further emigration. In 1891 the first Japanese immigrants landed on the United States mainland. From 1891 until 1900, 27,440 arrived on the West Coast and Alaska. Roughly two-thirds of them landed in California. They worked as fieldhands, domestics, railroad workers, miners, lumberjacks, in sawmills and fish canneries. The majority came from four southern districts, or prefectures, of Japan—Hiroshima, Yamaguchi, Wakayama, and Fukuoka.

These first immigrants, or *issei* (first generation), were almost all young men; about half were in their late teens and

The first waves of Japanese immigrants generally consisted of young men who came to work in Hawaii's fields, harvesting crops like sugarcane or pineapple.

twenties. Until 1908, Japanese women were prohibited from entering the United States. The average *issei* came with at least an eighth-grade education; some held college degrees. Many were students—*kugakusei* or *dekasegi shosei* (student laborers)—who came to America to learn English while earning money for college. Others were men whose families were suffering in Japan's rural depression, or whose businesses had failed.

The *issei* came to America with one goal in mind: to get rich and return to Japan. They were known as *dekaseginin* (temporary emigrant workers). America offered the promise of unlimited opportunities. Pamphlets published in Japan described the United States as a utopia where money grew on trees and gold was scattered in the streets.

The *issei* motto, *sannen ganbatte kaeru* (Work hard for three years and then return home), proved wildly unrealistic. In 1900, a farm worker earned $1.50 a day; a railroad worker, between $1.35 and $1.65 a day. In Hawaii, the average daily wage for Japanese workers was 65 cents. If they were brought to America by a labor contractor, they had to pay him a fee on top of their own expenses. So workers had precious little to show for their toil—certainly not the easy fortunes they had envisioned. Nonetheless, the first wave of *issei* sent roughly $3 million back to Japan, a phenomenal sum in those days.

Many *issei* started as migrant workers, constantly traveling wherever there were temporary jobs to be found. Railroad workers lived in boxcars that shuttled them from one construction site to another. Men sojourned to Alaska to work in the canneries during salmon season. Farm workers moved from farm to farm, carrying their own bedding; they were called *buranke katsugi* (blanket carriers).

Whether picking crops in southern California in 120-degree heat, or working on railroads in the Rockies in minus-20-degree winds, the *issei* endured severe hardships. Farmhands worked from dawn to dusk stooped over, hoeing weeds or picking crops. Cannery workers were cloaked in the stench of brine and fish that clung to their clothes and skin. Railroad gangs hoisted eight-foot-long railroad ties onto boxcars. Malnutrition, tuberculosis, and pneumonia were common.

Away from home for the first time, on their own in a foreign land, many of the young men were overcome with homesickness and loneliness. They took to drinking cheap or homemade liquor, which often made them violently ill. Night blindness, caused by drinking impure alcohol, was not unusual. Many men gambled or played pool and often wound up losing all of their hard-earned money.

But the *issei* were too ambitious to remain migrant workers and day laborers. By 1910, there were 3,000 *issei*-owned small businesses: dry goods stores, laundries, groceries, barbershops, cafes. At the same time, roughly 6,000 *issei* had earned enough to buy or lease their own farms. Although they worked only about 4 percent of California's farmland, they were growing more than 10 percent of its crops. In

First-generation Japanese immigrants acted on their ambitions and made great strides in their adopted country. In 1916, this young woman was studying dentistry in San Francisco.

1910, they grew 70 percent of California's strawberry yield. It was an *issei* farmer named Ikuta who raised California's first commercial crop of rice.

One of the most successful *issei* was Kinji Ushijima, who changed his name to George Shima. He came to California in 1887 and worked as a potato picker. Then he began to buy swampland in the San Joaquin Valley and convert it into fertile farmland. By 1912, he was growing potatoes on 10,000 acres. Dubbed the "Potato King," he became a leader of the Japanese American community. When he died, he was a multimillionaire.

Abiko Kyutaro was another successful *issei*. He arrived in San Francisco in 1885 with one dollar in his pocket. He worked menial jobs while attending school. During the 1890s, he operated several service businesses and launched a newspaper, the *Nichibei Shinbun*. Through his newspaper, he encouraged the *issei* to settle permanently in the United States. To further the cause, he bought 3,200 acres of farmland in Livingston, California, and sold forty-acre plots to Japanese farmers. This model community was called the Central California Land Company, or the Yamato Colony.

Another Yamato Colony was established in 1904 near Boca Raton, Florida, by Jo Sakai, a Japanese educated in the United States. He recruited colonists from his hometown of Miyazu, near Kyoto. After two years, they produced their first large pineapple crop. The colony expanded: More colonists arrived; a new railroad station and post office were built. But in 1908 a blight severely damaged the pineapple fields and the colony never recovered.

Gradually, the idea of settlement began to spread, as dreams of an easy fortune dissipated in the dust of dry, hot fields. Between 1901 and 1909, another 42,500 *issei* would arrive, joined by another 38,000 who came to the mainland from Hawaii. Unlike the first wave of immigrants, however, a significant portion of this second group consisted of women.

Picture Brides

It was not until after the "Gentlemen's Agreement," a 1907 treaty intended to curb Japanese immigration, that Japanese women began to arrive in the United States in force. By 1910, there were 5,600 Japanese women in America; by 1920, more than 22,000.

Many *issei* women came to the United States as "picture brides." These women exchanged pictures and letters with men living in the United States, usually through the arrangements of a broker. If a match was made, the couple were married in Japan in the absence of the bridegroom. Then the new bride traveled to the United States to join her husband.

The picture bride marriage (*shashin kekkon*) was susceptible to fraud. The majority of the women arrived ten years after the first wave of immigrants. Thus, wives were usually ten to fifteen years younger than their husbands. Some older men sent outdated photographs, or photographs of imposters. Many suitors exaggerated their situations. Fruit-stand vendors described themselves as large store owners, share-croppers, as landowners. Two-room shacks became mansions.

Even so, for the picture brides the United States represented a way out of the ordinary life. Japanese women at that time had few opportunities to pursue careers in Japan; society expected them to become good wives and mothers— and nothing else.

It was, to be sure, a perilous adventure. A picture bride was not only getting married, but moving halfway around the world. In the United States she was greeted by a complete stranger, probably much older than she expected, who introduced himself as her husband. Their first stop would have been at a clothing store, where she would be fitted with alien, painfully ill-fitting Western garments to replace the kimonos she had brought with her.

Poverty and backbreaking work likely awaited her. Home might be nothing more than a two-room shack with a dirt floor. She had no friends or acquaintances, could speak no

Thousands of Japanese women flocked to the United States as "picture brides," having been matched and married without ever meeting their husbands.

English. She might work as a domestic, or in the fields alongside her husband. If she had children, she would have to stay up late at night after the rest of the family went to bed, doing part-time work or household chores. To make ends meet, some women operated boardinghouses for *issei* bachelors.

One Japanese American woman recalled of her mother: "It was so unusual to see her rest . . . once when I saw her lying prone on the long wooden bench alongside the dining table in broad daylight, I thought she had died. It turned out that she was pregnant."[1]

Once they started marrying, settling down, and raising families, the *issei* started to think of the United States as home. They began to adopt American ways of life. Like true immigrants, they wanted to join American society. But their eager embrace of the country was not returned.

The Yellow Peril

The Chinese were the first Asian immigrants to the United States. When they first arrived in the 1850s, the western United States was still wilderness. The Chinese role in developing the West was crucial. The Chinese cleared the way for the intercontinental railroad, cleared land for farming, and mined precious metals. They worked the hardest, most dangerous jobs, and at much lower wages than American workers.

Because the Chinese were cheaper to hire, Americans saw them as a threat to their jobs. No minimum wage existed, so an employer paid as little as workers were willing to accept. By the 1870s labor unions, politicians, property owners, and journalists began to call for the exclusion of Chinese immigrants from America. Words turned into deeds. On September 2, 1885, a mob attacked and burned the Chinatown district in Rock Springs, Wyoming, killing twenty-eight Chinese and wounding fifteen. The rioters went unpunished.

While lost jobs and depressed wages were the usual

---

[1] Mei T. Nakano, *Japanese American Women* (Sebastopol, CA: Mina Press, 1990), p. 44.

complaints against the Chinese, racial fears underscored anti-Chinese sentiments. The Chinese, who did not speak English and dressed in the clothing of their homeland, were threatening simply because they were different, strange. In 1876 a prominent California farmer, Henry Larkin, put it bluntly: "This State should be a State for white men. . . . We want no other race here."[2] In 1882, the first Chinese Exclusion Act was passed, prohibiting Chinese immigration for the next sixty years.

When the *issei* first began arriving in the 1880s, they were welcomed by employers because they were willing to work for even less than the Chinese. Like the Chinese, the *issei* represented a source of cheap labor for employers and, as such, a threat to American-born workers. Before long the same complaints that had been made about the Chinese were being leveled at them.

In 1908, the Asiatic Exclusion League, a federation of local trade unions in San Francisco, published a statement that complained . . .

> the Japanese have a lower scale of living and possess peculiar qualities which make them offensive . . . they are able to exist in a manner with which a white man in the United States cannot compete. They can live with a minimum of creature comfort and require a small amount of food.[3]

What the proclamation does not mention, of course, is that the *issei* had little choice but to "live with a minimum of creature comfort" in the United States. They were simply able to survive extreme hardships—hardly a quality "peculiar" to the Japanese.

In 1904 the Hawaiian Sugar Planters Association passed a resolution barring Japanese and other Asian immigrants from

---

[2] Elmer Clarence Sandmeyer, *The Anti-Chinese Movement in California* (Urbana: University of Illinois Press, 1991), p. 70.

[3] *Proceedings of the Asiatic Exclusion League* (San Francisco: Allied Printing, 1908), p. 215.

holding higher-paying jobs. Japanese plantation workers there began to organize into unions and staged major strikes—in 1904, 1905, 1906, 1909, and 1920—protesting low wages and harsh treatment by their white overseers, whom they called the *luna* or *haole*.

The *issei*'s situation was complicated by events abroad. With its newly modernized military, Japan began to seize territories by force. It defeated China in the Sino-Japanese War of 1894–1895 and Russia ten years later in the Russo-Japanese War, for control of Formosa (now Taiwan), parts of China, and the Korean peninsula. Japanese aggression provoked distrust in the West; the defeat of Russia, an Old World power, by "upstart" Japan was especially jarring to Western nations.

In the United States, some politicians and journalists suspected the *issei* of being sent to prepare for a Japanese invasion of North America. California newspapers dubbed the imaginary crisis the "Yellow Peril." Rumors began to spread that Japanese farmers were poisoning their produce. *Issei* were assaulted, their homes vandalized, their businesses boycotted.

Japan's military expeditions in Asia alienated not only white Americans, but other Asian immigrants. In the resistance against Japanese forces that lasted from 1907 to 1909, 15,000 Koreans died. Korean immigrants in the United States boycotted Japanese goods and services and formed private military schools to train young men to fight Japan. Chinese immigrants also boycotted Japanese businesses after the Sino-Japanese War, and later, during World War I, when Japan tried to take even more land in China.

The Japanese government in turn blamed the Chinese for stirring up anti-Asian sentiments and tried to distance the *issei* from other immigrants. It discouraged them from gambling in Chinese-owned gambling parlors. Tensions between the *issei* and other immigrants rose when they competed for the same jobs.

In 1906 the San Francisco school board ordered the children of Japanese immigrants segregated from white children

The Sino-Japanese War sparked fears of Japanese aggression and inflamed tensions between Japanese Americans and other Asian immigrants. Here, Japanese soldiers leave a Chinese city with their loot.

into separate schools for Asians. The Japanese government strongly protested the move, which it saw as a blow to Japan's prestige. President Theodore Roosevelt pressured the board into rescinding its order. In return he negotiated the "Gentlemen's Agreement," which set limits on new immigrants, and stopped the migration of Japanese from Hawaii to the mainland.

Another source of friction between *issei* and Californians was property ownership. Once the *issei* began to settle down and buy land, the prospect of thousands of propertied Japanese frightened white citizens. Mayor James D. Phelan of San Francisco ran for state senate under the slogan KEEP CALIFORNIA WHITE.[4] In August 1913 California's Alien Land Law went into effect, which prohibited "aliens ineligible to citizenship" (namely, Asians) from owning land and limited any leases they held to three years.

The Alien Land Law had loopholes, however. Because their children, the *nisei* (second generation), were American citizens by birth, the laws did not apply to them; some *issei* farmers bought land in their children's names. But in 1920 and again in 1923, the law was changed to eliminate loopholes. So farmers entered into secret arrangements with landlords or formed corporations listing the names of citizens as owners, to buy land. Many *issei*, however, lost their farms and were forced to find new livelihoods.

The *issei* tried to fit into American society, changing many aspects of their life—their dress, their diet, their religion, their names. Despite their industry, their contributions to society, and their best efforts at adopting American ways of life, the *issei* could not overcome the distrust and hostility of people like James D. Phelan, who declared: "The Chinese and Japanese are not bona fide citizens. . . . They are not the stuff of which American citizens can be made."[5]

---

[4] Ronald Takaki, *Strangers from a Different Shore* (New York: Little, Brown, 1989), p. 204.

[5] Roger Daniels, *The Politics of Prejudice* (Berkeley: University of California Press, 1977), p. 21.

The prospect of Japanese land ownership incited white racism and led to the Alien Land Law of 1913, which basically prohibited Asian immigrants from buying land. Some farmers, however, managed to obtain land through loopholes in the system.

In October 1919, the Japanese consulate decided to stop granting visas to picture brides, in an attempt to placate the anti-Japanese movement. The move angered many *issei* without changing American attitudes. On July 20, 1921, 150 *issei* laborers were run out of town by a mob in Turlock, California. In twelve states, from Washington to Louisiana, alien land laws were passed.

When the *issei* turned to the U.S. Supreme Court for protection of their rights, it was unsympathetic. In 1922 it let stand the 1790 law that prohibited Japanese from naturalization. In three subsequent cases, *Porterfield v. Webb, Terrace v. Thompson,* and *Cockrill et al. v. People of State of California,* it upheld the alien land laws.

Finally, on May 26, 1924, President Calvin Coolidge signed an immigration bill banning all future Japanese immigration to the United States. It went into effect on July 1 and would remain in force until 1952.

The Bridge

On February 21, 1926, the *Rafu Shimpo*, a California-based newspaper for Japanese immigrants, published its first English-language edition. It included the following announcement:

> Our long-hoped-for wishes are materialized, and so here we have a medium to publish news of the second generation, for the second generation, and by the second generation.[6]

In 1900, there were approximately 270 *nisei*, or second generation, in America. By 1940, there were roughly 80,000. For the *issei*, their children the *nisei* represented a stabilizing force for the Japanese in America. As the *issei* began to have children, they settled down and gave up their migratory way of life. Gone, too, for *issei* fathers was the dream of returning to Japan as instant rich men.

Because the *nisei* were born on U.S. soil, they were American citizens. They had rights the *issei* did not. The *issei* hoped that the English-speaking, American-educated *nisei* would serve as a bridge between the *issei* and the rest of society. They worked hard to assure their children an education.

The problem with a bridge is that while linking two sides, it belongs to both sides and neither side at the same time. At school the *nisei* learned about the United States; at home they learned of Japan. They followed both Japanese and American customs. They ate peanut butter and jelly sandwiches for lunch, *tsukemono* and rice for dinner; celebrated Japanese New Year and Christmas; listened to their mothers singing Japanese love songs and swing bands playing on the radio. Some *nisei* westernized their first names for school and answered to their Japanese given names at home.

---

[6] Brian Niiya, ed., *Japanese American History* (New York: Facts on File, 1993), pp. 45–46.

Japanese American families, especially the second generation, struggled with the pressure to assimilate into mainstream American culture as well as the desire to hold on to certain aspects of Japanese culture.

Many *nisei* also attended two schools, public school followed by Japanese-language school. The dual instruction made some feel like two people. One woman recalled: "At Bailey Gatzert School I was a jumping, screaming, roustabout Yankee. . . . But Nihon Gakko [Japanese school] was so different. . . . I suddenly became a modest, faltering, earnest little Japanese girl with a small, timid voice."[7]

Eventually, though, the Japanese gave way to the American. Most *nisei* could barely speak Japanese, even with language school. This created a barrier, since most *issei* could speak only a little English. In many households, the parents spoke Japanese and the children responded in English. Their conversations were limited to the most basic notions and simplest subjects. Japanese ideals, attitudes, and traditions were incomprehensible to *nisei*.

---

[7] Takaki, *Strangers from a Different Shore*, p. 215.

Some parents sent their *nisei* children back to Japan for
education. These students, known as *kibei,* faced extremely
difficult dilemmas. Because of their U.S. citizenship and,
typically, their poor command of the Japanese language, they
were treated as foreigners in Japan. When they returned to
the United States, they were regarded much the same way
by their *nisei* peers.

Like most American children the *nisei* rebelled against
their parents. Ironically, the reasons the *issei* held such high
hopes for their children turned out to be the same reasons
they had trouble disciplining them: The *nisei* were American
citizens; the *issei* were not. The *nisei* had American
educations; the *issei* did not. The *nisei* could speak English;
the *issei,* for the most part, could not.

Adding to the difficulties were the differences in age. *Issei*
men did not begin to marry until 1908, when picture brides
were first allowed into the United States. By then most
husbands were in their thirties and forties. Some men did
not become fathers until they were almost in their fifties.
When many of the *nisei* were coming of age, their fathers
were old enough to be their grandfathers.

The *nisei* joined the larger society enthusiastically. They
competed in sports, took part in extracurricular activities,
joined scout troops and youth clubs. They excelled in school
and enjoyed success in areas that had been closed to their
parents. In 1930 three Hawaiian *nisei,* Tasaku Oka,
Masayoshi Yamashiro, and Noboru Miyake, became the first
Japanese Americans elected to public office.

The *nisei* made a conscious effort to demonstrate their
patriotism and civic-mindedness. In May 1923 *nisei* from
various parts of California formed the American Loyalty
League, whose mission was to promote good relations with
whites. Four years later, a *nisei* group, the New Americans,
was created. Both organizations were precursors to the Japanese American Citizens League (JACL), which was inaugu-
rated on August 29, 1930, in Seattle. The JACL was to play
an enormous role during the crisis that was looming on the
horizon—World War II.

The Road to War

On September 18, 1931, Japanese army officers in Manchuria blew up a strip of railroad and blamed it on Chinese. The Japanese government used the incident as an excuse to invade Manchuria. This marked the beginning of hostilities in the Pacific.

By 1937 Japan and China were at war. The rest of the world condemned Japan's actions. In response, Japan withdrew from the League of Nations, the precursor to the United Nations. Over the next four years relations between the United States and Japan deteriorated. President Franklin Roosevelt imposed an oil embargo on Japan and froze all Japanese-held assets in the United States.

While some Japanese Americans remained loyal to Japan, most allegiances were with the United States. In 1940 a *nisei* member of the JACL, Mike Masaoka, composed the "Japanese American Creed," which stated, among other things:

> I am proud that I am an American citizen of Japanese ancestry. . . . I pledge myself to do honor to [America] at all times and in all places; to support her Constitution; to obey her laws; to respect her flag; to defend her against all enemies, foreign or domestic. . . .[8]

A traditional Japanese saying goes: *Umi no oya yori mo sodate no oya* (Your adopted parents are your real parents). Ironically, taking the side of the United States against Japan was a very "Japanese" thing to do.

The two countries were on a collision course. It came on December 7, 1941, when the Japanese navy attacked the U.S. naval base at Pearl Harbor.

"A Jap Is a Jap"

In the fall of 1941, before Pearl Harbor, Curtis B. Munson, a State Department official, issued a report on the "Japanese

---

[8] Niiya, *Japanese American History*, p. 184.

The Japanese attack on the U.S. naval base in Pearl Harbor on December 7, 1941, led to anti-Japanese discrimination and hysteria.

American threat" on the West Coast. He found the threat nonexistent. The *nisei*, he noted, "are not Japanese in culture . . . they are not oriental or mysterious, they are very American."[9] He concluded:

> We do not believe that [Japanese Americans] would be at the least any more disloyal than any other racial group in the United States with whom we went to war.[10]

A subsequent memo to the President from the FBI director J. Edgar Hoover reached similar conclusions. Hoover ridiculed the military's "hysteria and lack of judgment" and noted one incident "where the power lines were sabotaged by cattle scratching their backs on the wires."[11]

But in the immediate aftermath of Pearl Harbor, hysteria was the norm. The Secretary of the Navy, Henry Knox, accused Japanese Americans in Hawaii of aiding the attack. In fact, many of them had come to the islands' defense.[12] Police and FBI searched homes and confiscated property ranging from fishing boats to toy guns. More than 2,000 *issei* were arrested without being charged with any crimes and held for months in camps, jails, and military bases.

Military leaders and politicians who argued for the removal of Japanese Americans prevailed. Among them were General John L. DeWitt of the Western Defense Command and California's Attorney General Earl Warren (the future Chief Justice of the Supreme Court). On February 19, 1942, President Franklin Roosevelt signed Executive Order 9066, which called for the "evacuation" and internment of "all persons of Japanese ancestry" on the West Coast.

The internment policy made little sense. Although Hawaii

---

[9] Michi Weglyn, *Years of Infamy* (New York: William Morrow, 1976), p. 48.

[10] Niiya, *Japanese American History*, p. 242.

[11] John Armor and Peter Wright, *Manzanaar* (New York: Times Books, 1988), p. 21.

[12] Commission on Wartime Relocation and Internment of Civilians, *Personal Justice Denied* (Washington, DC: U.S. Government Printing Office, 1982), p. 55.

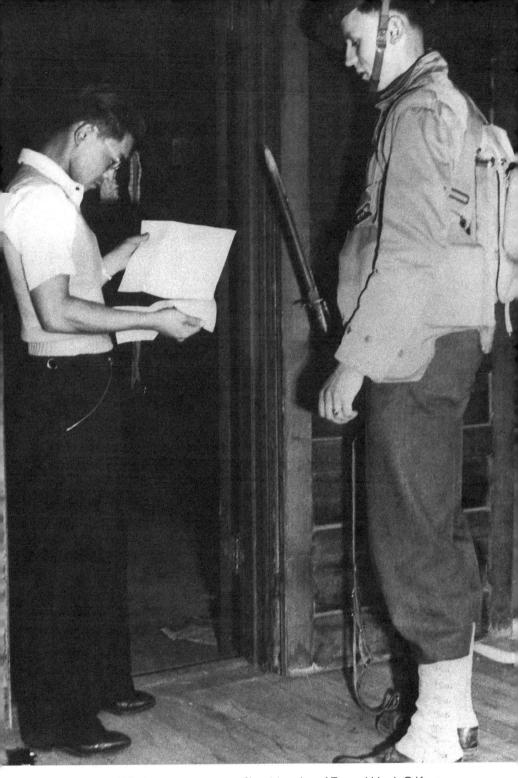

A private in the U.S. Army serves papers to Shiro Matsushita of Terminal Island, California, informing him that he and hundreds of other residents must leave the island for an internment camp.

had borne the brunt of the attack, no mass evacuation of Japanese Americans was ordered there. And while the United States was also at war with Germany and Italy, German Americans and Italian Americans were, for the most part, left alone.

On March 2, 1942, General DeWitt ordered the exclusion of Japanese Americans from parts of California, Oregon, Washington, and Arizona. On March 18, 1942, the Wartime Relocation Authority was created to run the internment camps. On March 24 the Army issued the first evacuation order to forty-five Japanese American families living on Bainbridge Island in Seattle, Washington.

By August 7, 1942, 106,770 people—about 70,000 of them American citizens—had reported to temporary assembly centers such as the Santa Anita racetrack. From there they were transferred to ten permanent "relocation centers" in six western states and Arkansas, where they were held prisoner until shortly before the war's end.

Most Japanese Americans cooperated with the authorities, and no acts of sabotage or espionage by Japanese Americans were ever reported. Still they were considered dangerous. General DeWitt justified the internment to Congress with a curious twist of logic: "The very fact that no sabotage has taken place is a disturbing and confirming indication that such action will be taken."[13]

Early in the war the threat of a Japanese invasion seemed real to the residents of the West Coast: The Pacific fleet had almost been wiped out. Fear revived old hatreds; it was the "Yellow Peril" all over again. California newspaper columnist Henry McLemore wrote: "Personally, I hate the Japanese. And that goes for all of them."[14]

The racial attitudes of the day made it hard for people to distinguish Japanese from Japanese Americans. Although the *issei* had been in America for more than half a century and

---

[13] *Personal Justice Denied*, p. 82.
[14] Bill Hosogawa, *Nisei: The Quiet Americans* (New York: William Morrow, 1969), p. 265.

The evacuation of Japanese Americans to internment camps during World War II was a devastating blow to the many who had worked hard to become part of American society. The expressions on the faces of this family illustrate the shock of having all they had worked for taken away.

In Parkville, Missouri, Japanese American students continued their studies at Park College despite community protests during the tense aftermath of Pearl Harbor. Here, they take part in a flag-raising ceremony.

the *nisei* were native-born citizens, to many people they were no different from the pilots who bombed Pearl Harbor. In his testimony to Congress, DeWitt made the remark for which he is best remembered: "A Jap is a Jap."

Voices of Dissent

Though the evacuation and internment of Japanese Americans is now recognized as a grave injustice, at the time the vast majority of Americans supported President Roosevelt's decision. Hatred of Japan for the attack on Pearl Harbor ran high, and few people were willing to speak up for the rights of Japanese Americans. Newspaper columnist Westbrook Pegler wrote: "The Japanese in California should be under guard to the last man and woman right now and to hell with habeas corpus until the danger is over."[15]

Habeas corpus is a Latin phrase meaning "produce the body." It refers to a fundamental tenet of our system of laws: that one cannot be arrested and imprisoned unless charged with a specific crime. The Japanese Americans interned during World War II were never charged with any crimes. Their only "crime," as it were, was being born of Japanese ancestry.

A small minority dissented, however. On December 8, 1941, the day after Pearl Harbor, Congressman John Coffee of Washington in the House of Representatives made what was surely an unpopular speech at the time:

> It is my fervent hope and prayer that residents of the United States of Japanese extraction will not be made the victims of pogroms directed by self-proclaimed patriots and by hysterical self-anointed heroes.... Let us not make a mockery of our Bill of Rights by mistreating these folks.[16]

Unfortunately, his courageous plea for reason fell on deaf ears.

---

[15] Hosogawa, *Nisei: The Quiet Americans*, p. 265.
[16] Ibid., p. 266.

Other prominent dissenters included Congressmen Bertrand Gearhart and H. Jerry Voorhis of California, Richard Gordon Sproul and Monroe E. Deutsch, President and Provost of the University of California, respectively, and U.S. Army General Mark Clark. As early as 1942 Clark knew that the evacuation was unnecessary because Japan would never be able to invade North America. He eventually became a prominent figure in the history of Japanese Americans as a commander of the all-*nisei* 100th Battalion and 442nd Regimental Combat Team in the Europe theater of World War II.

Church groups also went against the tide of popular opinion to lend support to Japanese American internees. The Federal Council of Churches and the Home Missions Council voiced their opposition to the internment. The American Friends Service Committee (more commonly known as the Quakers) donated educational materials to the internment camps and lobbied the government to allow *nisei* to attend college outside the camps. It also provided invaluable financial aid to *nisei* college students. The American Baptist Home Mission Society helped Japanese Americans secure their property during the evacuation and later aided in their resettlement after the war.

One extraordinary man who rose above the prejudice of the day was a Mississippi cattle rancher by the name of Earl Finch. When *nisei* men volunteered for military duty, they were sent to Hattiesburg, Mississippi, for basic training. The majority of people in Hattiesburg regarded them with distrust and hostility. Finch, by contrast, became the *nisei* soldiers' self-appointed godfather. While they were in boot camp he arranged dances, parties, even trips to New Orleans for them. Later in the war, he visited the wounded in hospitals across the country. After the internment camps closed at the war's end, he helped many of the veterans and their families to leave the camps and resettle.

Internment

The Japanese Americans became, in effect, prisoners of war and were treated as such. People were given as little as four days to evacuate their homes. They could take with them only what they could carry. Homes, cars, heirlooms were sold for a pittance, abandoned, or stolen. Japanese Americans lost approximately $77 million in property and income in the evacuation.[17] Today it would be worth more than $6 billion.

Lost, too, was the goodwill in the communities that had been built over many years. Homes were looted and vandalized, and property was stolen by neighbors and business associates. Friendships were torn apart. In his poem "From Our Album" Lawson Fusao Inada writes of Jimmy, his father's German shepherd, who "wouldn't eat after the evacuation . . . [or] live with another master / and pined away, skin and bone."[18]

In the assembly centers, the evacuees themselves were treated not much better than animals. At Santa Anita racetrack, evacuees were housed in old horse stables that reeked of manure. As many as three families were crammed into single stalls and slept on sacks filled with straw. The toilets were communal, and the old horses' showers had only a low partition dividing the men's and women's sections. Doctors and nurses had little more than aspirin and rubbing alcohol on hand to treat the ill.

The relocation centers, which the WRA called "pioneer communities," were in effect prisons. Barbed wire fences and armed guard towers ringed the camps. Families lived in barracks; as many as eight people shared a single room. Long lines for meals, showers, and the bathroom were parts of everyday life. In summer months barracks were sweltering by day, frigid by night.

The residents tried to keep up a semblance of normal life in the camps. Children went to schools, many taught by visiting teachers (the Quakers and Methodists were among the few groups in the United States sympathetic to Japanese Americans). People worked in camp jobs, planted gardens,

---

[17] *Personal Justice Denied*, p. 119.

[18] Lawson Fusao Inada, *Before the War* (New York: William Morrow, 1971), p. 15.

tried to decorate their grim barracks. Camp newspapers were published. But perhaps the main enemy of the evacuees was overwhelming boredom.

To escape the tedium of camp life, some *nisei* took jobs as temporary farm workers. Labor was in short supply during the war, so they were allowed to leave the camps temporarily to harvest crops. Seabrook Farms in New Jersey was a major employer of *nisei* during the war. *Nisei* were also credited with saving the sugar beet crop in Montana one year. As the war progressed, more and more were furloughed out of the camps to help in the war effort.

But tensions inevitably developed in the camps. Families began to disintegrate as parents lost control over their children. Factions formed between those who wished to cooperate with the government and those who did not. One divisive issue was a WRA loyalty questionnaire that was handed out in 1943. Two questions were particularly troubling:

#27. Are you willing to serve in the armed forces of the United States on combat duty wherever ordered?

#28. Will you swear unqualified allegiance to the United States of America . . . and forswear any form of allegiance or obedience to the Japanese emperor, to any other foreign government, power, or organization?

Question 27 applied to the *nisei*: Why should they fight for a country that was holding them and their families prisoner? Question 28 posed a problem for the *issei*. They were asked to give up their Japanese citizenship, but they were not allowed to become American citizens. By answering yes they would become, in effect, people without a country.

Those who answered no to both questions or did not answer at all were branded "disloyal" and transferred to the camp at Tule Lake, Arizona, which was converted into a maximum security prison. *Nisei* who answered yes to both questions were soon called upon to serve their country.

Nisei who volunteered for military service were rejected as "enemy aliens" until President Roosevelt ordered the army to induct *nisei* soldiers in 1943. In Hawaii, Second Lieutenant Robert Kadowaki receives an aloha lei from Florence Shirotakei.

"Go for Broke"

On December 7, *nisei* who belonged to Hawaii's National Guard were called to duty and stood alongside regular army units ready to defend the islands from Japanese invasion. The next month they were discharged from the Guard because of their Japanese ancestry. On the mainland *nisei* who volunteered for military service were designated "4C" (enemy aliens) by the draft board and rejected.

The JACL and other groups lobbied the government to allow *nisei* to serve in the military. Finally, on January 22, 1943, President Roosevelt ordered the army to induct *nisei* soldiers. The 442nd Regimental Combat Team was made up of *nisei* from the mainland and combined with the 100th Hawaiian National Guard Battalion. The two units were sent to Europe in 1944. *Nisei* who could speak Japanese also served in the Pacific with the Military Intelligence Service as translators, interpreters, and interrogators. Out of 36,000 eligible *nisei*, roughly 33,000 took part in the war.[19] The 100th/442nd became one of the most highly decorated units in the United States Army. It won more than 3,900 citations for bravery. It suffered one of the highest casualty rates as well, as it was usually sent where the fighting was fiercest. "Go for broke," a gamblers' phrase from Hawaii, became the outfit's motto. After the war, President Harry Truman honored the 100th/442nd at a White House ceremony. He said: "You fought for the free nations of the world. . . . You fought not only the enemy, you fought prejudice, and you have won."

"We Don't Serve Japs"

Truman may have been overly optimistic. When the government began closing the relocation centers on January 1, 1945, it was the beginning of another war for many evacuees and veterans returning from Europe. Captain (later Senator) Daniel K. Inouye, who lost his right arm in combat, tried to get a haircut in San Francisco. He was told by the barber: "We don't serve Japs here." When the family of Kazuo Masuda, a *nisei* soldier killed in action, tried to return to their home in Santa Ana, California, they were harassed and threatened by local residents.

The evacuees' relief at being released from the camps conflicted with their fear of what awaited them on the outside. At train stations they saw signs NO JAPS ALLOWED and NO JAPS WELCOME. Many people found their homes vandalized and their fields ruined; everything they had worked for was gone. Some of the older *issei* never made it home and died in the camps.

One of the results of the internment was the dispersal, or diaspora, of Japanese Americans throughout the United States. Before the war the vast majority of Japanese Americans were living on the West Coast and in Hawaii. By war's

---

[19] Masayo Umezawa Duus, *Unlikely Liberators* (Honolulu: University of Hawaii Press, 1987), p. 231.

end many began to resettle in the Midwest, the East Coast, and the Southeast.

In 1980, nearly forty years after Pearl Harbor, Congress established a Commission on Wartime Relocation and Internment of Civilians. It found that there had been no justification for the internment and recommended that the government offer an apology and payment of damages to the former evacuees. A reparations bill was signed by President Ronald Reagan in 1988.

The chief sponsors of the bill in Congress were three *nisei*: Senators Inouye and the late Masayuki "Spark" Matsunaga of Hawaii and Representative Robert Matsui of California.

After the War

By the 1960s the internment seemed like a distant memory. *Nisei* were working as doctors, lawyers, engineers, members of Congress. The average family income of Japanese Americans was nearly 32 percent higher than the national average. One out of two *sansei* (third-generation) children attended college. Many *nisei* did not talk about the internment to their children; they wanted to put the past behind them.

Like the *nisei* before them, the *sansei* had trouble understanding their parents' way of thinking. During the internment, a phrase commonly heard in the camps was *Shikata ga nai* (It can't be helped). The majority of evacuees accepted their situation with a minimum of complaint and tried to make the best of it. In Japan this attitude is known as *gaman*.

For many in the postwar generations, *gaman* was incomprehensible. Those who grew up in the 1960s and 1970s watched the protests against the Vietnam War and the Watergate hearings on television. They learned to be more questioning of authority and more outspoken than their parents and grandparents. A group of five *sansei* lawyers reopened the cases of Gordon Hirabayashi, Fred Korematsu, and Min Yasui, who had been convicted of violating the exclusion order during World War II. Yasui died before his

Kinjiro Matsudaira became the first Japanese American mayor in the United States when the city of Edmonton, Maryland, elected him in 1927.

case was decided; the convictions of Hirabayashi and Korematsu for violating the evacuation order were thrown out.

Success Stories

Though they make up only a small portion of the population, Japanese Americans have had a significant impact on this country in a variety of fields.

In the world of art, *issei* painter and photographer Yasuo Kuniyoshi (1889–1953) was a highly respected artist and much beloved art teacher in New York City from the 1920s until 1953. The sculptures and gardens of *nisei* artist Isamu Noguchi (1904–1988) are renowned throughout the world. A *nisei* architect from Seattle, Minoru Yamasaki (1912–1986), designed the World Trade Center in New York City. Woodworker George Nakashima is internationally recognized for his unique furniture pieces. More recently, the Japanese American artist Masami Teraoka won acclaim for

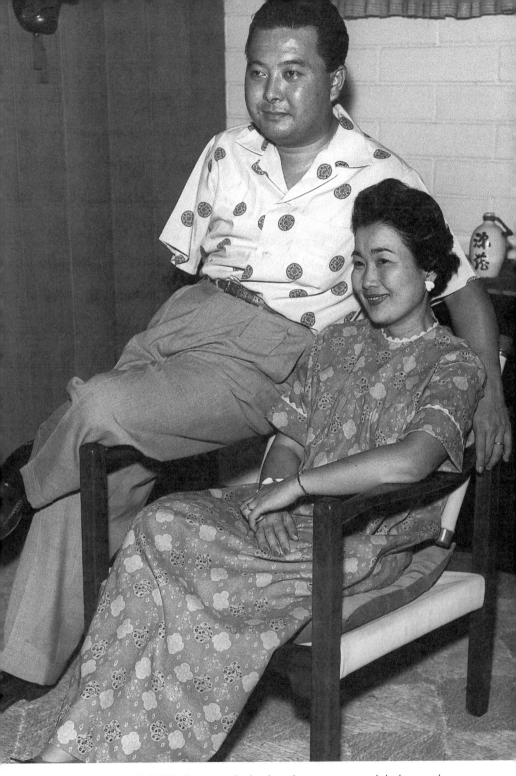

Daniel K. Inouye, a World War II veteran who lost his right arm in action in Italy, became the first U.S. senator of Japanese descent in 1959. Shown here with his wife, Margaret, he represents the state of Hawaii.

his "AIDS Series: Makiki Heights Disaster," a screen painting that uses traditional Japanese art forms to depict the AIDS crisis.

The contributions of Japanese Americans to the fields of science and medicine date back to the nineteenth century. Dr. Jokichi Takamine (1854–1922), an *issei* chemist, came to the United States in 1884 to study the hormone adrenaline. A philanthropist in his later years, he founded the Japanese Association of New York and aided other *issei* in their studies of chemistry, art, and music. Hideyo Noguchi (1876–1928), an *issei* scientist, came to the University of Pennsylvania in 1899 and achieved renown for his research in yellow fever and syphilis. He died of yellow fever in Africa while studying the disease. In 1985, Ellison Shoji Onizuka (1946–1986) became the first Japanese American to fly in space, as an astronaut aboard the shuttle *Discovery*. In 1986, he was killed along with six other crew members when the shuttle *Challenger* exploded.

Since 1930 Japanese Americans have been active in local, state, and national government. The late S. I. Hayakawa (1906–1992) and Masayuki "Spark" Matsunaga (1916–1990) both served in the U.S. Senate. Daniel K. Inouye is currently the U.S. senator from Hawaii. California's Robert Takeo Matsui and Norman Yoshio Mineta served in the U.S. Congress. Patsy Takemoto Mink, U.S. Congresswoman from Hawaii, became the first Asian American woman elected to Congress. George Ryoichi Ariyoshi became the first Japanese American governor. He served as Hawaii's governor from 1973 to 1986, the longest term in the state's history. In the judicial branch, Judge Lance Ito became known throughout the world for presiding over the trial of O. J. Simpson from 1994 to 1995.

Many Japanese American actors have enjoyed highly successful careers. George Takei, who is most famous for his role as Mr. Sulu in the *Star Trek* movies and television series, is also a Shakespearean actor, film star, writer, and political activist. California native Noriyuki "Pat" Morita, a veteran television and film actor, received an Academy

Award nomination in 1984 for his role in the movie *The Karate Kid.* Los Angeles-born actress Nobu McCarthy, who starred in the films *Farewell to Manzanaar* and *The Karate Kid,* is director of the East West Players, an Asian American theater group. One of the newest Japanese American actors is Tamlyn Tomita, whose films include *Come See the Paradise, The Joy Luck Club,* and *Picture Bride.*

A number of Japanese American athletes have achieved world class status. Weightlifter Harold Sakata won the silver medal at the 1948 summer Olympics in London, England. Four years later swimmers Ford Konno and Oyakawa Yoshinobu and weightlifter Tamio "Tommy" Kono all won gold medals at the Helsinki, Finland, Olympics. Forty years after that Kristi Yamaguchi won the gold medal in figure skating at the winter Olympics in Albertville, France. Other notable athletes include James Yoshinori Sakamoto (1903–1955), a featherweight boxer who later became a successful newspaper publisher; and major league baseball player Len Sakata, who played for the Baltimore Orioles and the New York Yankees.

Successful Japanese American writers are too numerous to be listed here. Many can be found in the *Resources* lists at the end of each chapter.

Resources

GENERAL REFERENCES—JAPAN

Beasley, W. G., ed. *Modern Japan: Aspects of History, Literature, and Society.* Berkeley: University of California Press, 1975.

A collection of essays on Japanese culture and history from the Meiji era (1868–1912) to the 1970s. Some of the essays on "modern" Japan may be dated, but the historical essays are always useful.

Bowring, Richard, and Kornicki, Peter, eds. *The Cambridge Encyclopedia of Japan.* Cambridge, U.K. and New York: Cambridge University Press, 1993.

An illustrated encyclopedia of all things Japanese, from *manga* (comic books) to Shintoism. Maps, glossary, bibliography.

Goedertier, Joseph M. *A Dictionary of Japanese History.* New York: Weatherhill, 1968.

A reference guide to important names, places, and dates in Japanese history. Somewhat dated, but still useful for the history up to World War II.

Hane, Mikiso. *Japan: A Historical Survey.* New York: Charles Scribner's Sons, 1972.

A comprehensive general history of Japan from the fourth century to the post-World War II economic miracle. Maps, glossary, bibliography, index.

———. *Peasants, Rebels, and Outcasts: The Underside of Modern Japan.* New York: Pantheon, 1982.

Using diaries, memoirs, fiction, documents, and personal accounts, Hane gives an account of what it was like to be an ordinary Japanese from the Meiji Restoration of 1868 to the years after World War II.

Hunter, Janet E. *Concise Dictionary of Modern Japanese History.* **Berkeley: University of California Press, 1982.**

A dictionary of important people, places, and events in modern Japanese history, from the Meiji Restoration (1868) to the 1980s. Appendices, maps.

Japan: An Illustrated Encyclopedia, **2 vols. Tokyo and New York: Kodansha, 1993.**

An encyclopedia of Japan with 11,000 entries and 4,000 illustrations. Topics include history, culture, natural history, society, sports, food, and more. It also features a chronology of Japanese history and a selected reading list.

Latourette, Kenneth Scott. *The History of Japan.* **New York: Macmillan, 1957.**

Originally written in 1918 and revised after World War II, this is a history of Japan from its mythological origins to its defeat in World War II.

Livingston, Jon; Moore, Joe; and Oldfeather, Felicia. *The Japan Reader,* **2 vols. New York: Pantheon, 1973.**

A sampler of essays, articles, public documents, and other writings that offer a comprehensive picture of Japanese history from 1800 to the 1970s, the decade of the so-called "economic miracle" when Japan became one of the richest nations in the world. Volume 1 covers the years 1800 to 1945; volume 2 is from 1945 to 1973.

Perkins, Dorothy. *Encyclopedia of Japan.* **New York: Facts on File, 1991.**

More than 1,000 entries on all aspects of Japan, from art to history to sports.

Powers, Richard G., and Kato, Hidetoshi. *Handbook of Japanese Culture.* **Westport, CT: Greenwood Press, 1989.**

A collection of twelve essays on modern Japan's popular culture—music, television, movies, sports, literature, religions, and more.

Reischauer, Edwin O. *Japan: The Story of a Nation,* **3d ed. New York: Alfred A. Knopf, 1981.**

A concise history of Japan, from the seventh century to the present day, with discussions of its language, culture, and religions. The late Reischauer was the leading American expert on Japan.

———. *The Japanese Today: Change and Continuity.* **Cambridge, MA: Harvard University Press, 1988.**

A portrait of the Japanese people and their lives in contemporary Japan.

Sansom, George. *A History of Japan,* **3 vols. Stanford, CA: Stanford University Press, 1958–63.**

A classic study of the origins of Japan as a nation-state from the 1300s to the Meiji Restoration of 1867.

———. *Japan: A Short Cultural History.* **Stanford, CA: Stanford University Press, 1978.**

Covering the same period as *A History of Japan*, Sansom examines the development of religion, arts, and literature.

CLASSICAL AND TRADITIONAL JAPANESE LITERATURE

Allyn, John. *The 47 Ronin Story.* **Rutland, VT: Charles E. Tuttle, 1970.**

A novel based on the famous Japanese legend of the forty-seven *ronin* (*samurai* not in the service of any master) who avenge the unjust death of their late master.

Basho, Matsuo. *On Love and Barley: Haiku of Basho.* **Translated by Lucien Stryk. New York: Penguin, 1986.**

A collection of *haiku* (short poems) by one of Japan's greatest poets. These poems chronicle his wanderings through the countryside of seventeenth-century Japan, celebrating nature and everyday experience.

Levy, Ian Hideo, ed. and tr. *The 10,000 Leaves* **(Manyoshu), vol. 1. Princeton, NJ: Princeton University Press, 1981.**

First of a planned four-volume set of the first and greatest anthology of Japanese classical poetry. This volume collects the poetry of the seventh and eighth centuries.

McCullough, Helen Craig, tr. *Tale of the Heike* **(Heike Monogatari). Stanford, CA: Stanford University Press, 1988.**

The epic tale of the civil wars that wracked Japan during the Heian period (twelfth century).

Murasaki, Shikibu. *Tale of Genji.* **Translated and abridged by Edward G. Seidensticker. New York: Vintage, 1992.**

The world's first novel, *Genji* is the story of the romantic adventures of a young nobleman, the son of the Japanese emperor, in tenth-century Japan.

Ono no Komachi. *The Ink Dark Moon: Poems of Ono no Komachi.* **Translated by Jane Hirshfield and Mariko Aratani. New York: Vintage, 1990.**

Ono was a noblewoman and legendary beauty who lived in the ninth century and, according to legend, died a beggar. Her poems are primarily about the pains and joys of love and passion.

Pekarik, Anthony J., ed. and tr. *Thirty-six Immortal Woman Poets.* **Illustrated by Chobunsai Eishi. New York: Georges Braziller, 1991.**

A collection of the works of women writers who flourished in Japan's aristocratic society from the ninth to the thirteenth centuries.

Sato, Hiroaki, and Watson, Burton, eds. and trs. *From the Country of Eight Islands: An Anthology of Japanese Poetry.* **New York: Columbia University Press, 1994.**

An anthology of Japanese poetry throughout the ages.

Shonagon, Sei. *The Pillow Book of Sei Shonagon.* **Translated by Ivan Morris. New York: Columbia University Press, 1991.**

Sei Shonagon was a court lady born in the tenth century. Her Pillow Book, a journal of sorts, gives a detailed portrait of life in the Heian aristocracy.

Tyler, Royall, ed. and tr. *Japanese Tales.* **New York: Pantheon, 1988.**

A collection of 220 tales, fables, jokes, and legends from medieval Japan.

Yamaguchi, Seishi. *Essence of Modern Haiku: 300 Poems.* **Atlanta, GA: Mangajin Books, 1991.**

A bilingual collection of 300 original *haiku*, with instructive commentary on the form.

TWENTIETH-CENTURY FICTION BY JAPANESE AUTHORS

Abe, Kobo. *Woman in the Dunes.* **Translated by E. Dale Saunders. New York: Vintage, 1990.**

The story of a scientist on a seaside vacation who is kidnapped by the residents of a remote coastal village and forced to work as a slave, alongside a mysterious, silent woman.

Birnbaum, Alfred, ed. *Monkey Brain Sushi: New Tastes in Japanese Fiction.* **Tokyo and New York: Kodansha, 1991.**

An anthology of short stories by contemporary Japanese authors. Gives a valuable portrait of present-day Japan.

Endo, Shusaku. *Silence.* **Translated by William Johnson. New York: Taplinger, 1990.**

The story of a seventeenth-century Portuguese missionary to Japan who is persecuted by authorities for his religion and nationality.

Hibbett, Howard, ed. *Contemporary Japanese Literature: An Anthology of Fiction, Film, and Other Writings Since 1945.* **Various translators. New York: Alfred A. Knopf, 1986.**

A collection of stories, plays, and screenplays by twenty-two modern Japanese authors.

Ibuse, Masuji. *Black Rain.* **Translated by John Bester. Tokyo and New York: Kodansha, 1969.**

Set in Japan immediately after World War II, a story of the victims of the atomic bombing of Hiroshima.

Ishiguro, Kazuo. *An Artist of the Floating World.* **New York: Vintage, 1992.**

Ishiguro, born in Japan but raised in England, is best known for his novel *The Remains of the Day,* the basis of the acclaimed movie. *Artist* is set in postwar Japan, and tells the story of a disgraced artist who created propaganda for the Japanese military during World War II.

————. *A Pale View of the Hills.* **New York: Vintage, 1992.**

Ishiguro's first novel, the story of a Japanese woman haunted by the suicide of her daughter and her own memories of the horrors of the atomic bombing of Nagasaki during World War II.

Kawabata, Yasunari. *The Old Castle*. Translated by J. Martin Holman. San Francisco: North Point, 1987.

By Japan's first winner of the Nobel Prize for Literature, the story of Chieko, the adopted daughter of loving parents who makes a startling discovery about her origins.

Mishima, Yukio. *The Sound of Waves*. Translated by Meredith Weatherby. New York: Vintage, 1994.

Set in a remote fishing village in Japan, a story of first love between a young fisherman and the daughter of a wealthy man.

Murakami, Haruki. *A Wild Sheep Chase*. Translated by Alfred Birnbaum. Tokyo and New York: Kodansha, 1989.

Set in contemporary Japan, a farcical detective story about a man hired to find a rare sheep that may or may not exist and may hold the key to Japan's future.

Oe, Kenzaburo. *The Silent Cry*. Translated by John Bester. Tokyo and New York: Kodansha, 1974.

By the winner of the 1994 Nobel Prize for Literature—the only Japanese writer besides Kawabata to win the award—the story of the complex relationship between two brothers who return to their ancestral home, a remote village in rural Japan.

Oka, Shihei. *Fires on the Plain*. Translated by Ivan Morris. Rutland, VT: Charles E. Tuttle, 1992.

Set in the Phillipines in the latter days of World War II, when Japan was on its way to defeat, *Fires* depicts the suffering of Japanese soldiers who were ordered to fight to the death.

Soseki, Natsume. *Botchan*. Translated by Alan Turney. Tokyo and New York: Kodansha, 1992.

The story of a young schoolteacher in a remote country school who runs up against its rules and conventions.

————. *I Am a Cat.* **Translated by Aiko Ito and Graeme Wilson. Rutland, VT: Charles E. Tuttle, 1986.**

Through the eyes of a housecat, the book takes a satiric look at the follies of humankind, demonstrated by the conversations that take place in the family's study.

Tanizaki, Junichiro. *The Makioka Sisters.* Translated by Edward G. Seidensticker. New York: Perigee, 1981.

The story of four sisters who have been raised in the traditions of aristocratic Japan and must face the changing realities of post-World War II society.

————. *Naomi.* **Translated and with an introduction by Anthony H. Chambers. San Francisco: North Point Press, 1990.**

Set in staid Tokyo in the 1920s, the story of a spirited young girl who defies the conventions and prohibitions of Japanese society.

Tsushima, Yuko. *Woman Running in the Mountains.* Translated by Geraldine Harcourt. New York: Pantheon, 1991.

Set in contemporary Japan, it tells the story of Takiko, a pregnant single woman who defies social convention and learns to fend for herself and her child.

JAPANESE AMERICAN HISTORY

Daniels, Roger. *Asian Americans: Chinese and Japanese in the United States Since 1850.* Seattle: University of Washington Press, 1988.

A general account of the immigration of Chinese and Japanese from the mid-nineteenth century to the present day.

Hosokawa, Bill, and Wilson, Robert A. *East to America: A History of the Japanese in the United States.* **New York: William Morrow, 1980.**

A narrative account of the experiences of three generations of Japanese Americans, from the late nineteenth century to modern times.

Namias, June. *First Generation: In the Words of Twentieth-Century American Immigrants*, **rev. ed. Foreword by Robert Coles. Urbana: University of Illinois Press, 1992.**

An oral history consisting of thirty-one interviews with first- and second-generation immigrants from Europe, Asia, Latin America, and the Caribbean.

Niiya, Brian, ed. *Japanese American History: An A-to-Z Reference from 1868 to the Present.* **New York: Facts on File, 1992.**

Compiled with the assistance of the Japanese American National Museum in Los Angeles, this is a comprehensive encyclopedia of all facets of Japanese American history.

Patterson, William. *Japanese Americans: Oppression and Success.* **New York: Random House, 1971.**

A discussion of Japanese Americans, their hardships and achievements.

Reischauer, Edwin O. *Japan: The Story of a Nation*, **3d ed. New York: Alfred A. Knopf, 1981.**

A concise history of Japan, from the seventh century to the present day, with discussions of its language, culture, and religions, by the leading American scholar of Japan.

THE *ISSEI* AND THE PACIFIC CROSSING

Nonfiction
Conroy, Hilary F. *The Japanese Frontier in Hawaii,*

1868–1898. Berkeley and Los Angeles: University of California Press, 1953.

Studies the initial Japanese emigration and the circumstances that helped make it possible, such as the recruitment of workers by sugar plantation owners.

Daniels, Roger. *The Politics of Prejudice.* **Berkeley: University of California Press, 1977.**

A history of the anti-Japanese movement in California from its beginnings in the late nineteenth century until the passage of the Asian Exclusion Act of 1924.

Ichioka, Yuji. *"Amerika-Nadeshiko:* **Japanese Immigrant Women in the United States, 1900–1924."** *Pacific Historical Review*, **Vol. 44, 1980, pp. 339–357.**

Portrays Japanese immigrant women in the United States during the early twentieth century. Describes the lives of picture brides. The influx of picture brides sparked controversy among anti-Japanese leaders, who saw the formation of Japanese American families as a threat.

———. "The Early Japanese Immigrant Quest for Citizenship: The Background of the 1922 Ozawa Case." *Amerasia Journal*, **Vol. 4, No. 2, 1977, pp. 1–22.**

Details the case of Takao Ozawa, an early Japanese immigrant who was denied naturalization in the United States because of his racial origins. Before the ruling, some Japanese Americans had managed to become naturalized, but they lost this status after the ruling in Ozawa's case was handed down.

———. *The Issei: The World of the First Generation Japanese Immigrants, 1885–1924.* **New York: The Free Press, 1988.**

An account of the exodus of the *issei* to the United States, their settlement in this country, and their struggles against exclusion from American shores.

Irwin, Yukiko, and Conroy, Hilary F. *East Across the Pacific: Historical and Sociological Studies of Japanese Immigration and Assimilation.* **Edited by Hillary Conroy and Scott Miyakawa. Santa Barbara: ABC-Clio Press, 1972.**

A scholarly work analyzing the Japanese immigration and assimilation process, focusing on historical and sociological aspects.

Ito, Kazuo. *Issei: A History of Japanese Immigrants in North America.* **Translated by Shinichiro Nakamura and Jean S. Gerard. Seattle: Executive Committee for the Publication of *Issei*, 1973.**

The history of the *issei* in North America. The *issei* paved the way for later generations of Japanese Americans.

Iwata, Masakazu. "The Japanese Immigrants in California Agriculture." *Agricultural History*, **Vol. 36, 1962, pp. 25–37.**

A concise description of Japanese American agricultural achievements in California. Japanese Americans found California's agricultural economy more conducive to advancement than the Hawaiian plantation system. Many went on to become farm owners and operators.

Kawakami, Barbara F. *Japanese Immigrant Clothing in Hawaii, 1885–1941.* **Honolulu: University of Hawaii Press, 1993.**

This book tells the story of two generations of plantation workers as revealed by the clothing they brought with them and the adaptations they made to the harsh conditions of their work.

————. *Promises Kept: The Life of an Issei Man.* New York: Chandler & Sharpe, 1991.

The story of the author's father and his struggles to provide for his thirteen children.

————. *Through Harsh Winters: The Life of a Japanese Immigrant Woman.* New York: Chandler & Sharpe, 1981.

A companion book to *Promises Kept,* the story of the author's mother and her own early struggles in America.

Lai, Him Mark; Lim, Genny; and Yung, Judy. *Island: Poetry and History of Chinese Immigrants on Angel Island, 1910–1940.* Seattle: University of Washington Press, 1980.

While it is concerned mainly with Chinese immigrants, *Island* gives valuable information about the immigration station on Angel Island in San Francisco Bay, the Ellis Island of the West Coast, where thousands of immigrants from Asia first arrived.

Modell, John. "The Japanese American Family: A Perspective for Future Research." *Pacific Historical Review,* Vol. 37, 1968, pp. 67–81.

An overview of Japanese American family life. Restrictions on immigration hindered the development of families for many early Japanese immigrants.

Moriyama, Alan Takeo. *Imingaisha: Japanese Emigration Companies and Hawaii.* Honolulu: University of Hawaii Press, 1985.

Many Japanese emigrants came to the United States with assistance from private companies that, for various fees, helped with applications, obtaining passports, and more. Here, Moriyama examines the role of these companies in the Japanese immigration to Hawaii.

Ogawa, Dennis M., with Glen Grant. *Kodomo no tame ni* **(For the sake of the children):** *The Japanese American Experience in Hawaii.* **Foreword by Lawrence H. Fuchs. Honolulu: University of Hawaii Press, 1978.**

A collection of essays about the lives of Japanese Americans in Hawaii, from the first waves of immigrants to young people today.

Sandmeyer, Elmer Clarence. *The Anti-Chinese Movement in California.* **Urbana: University of Illinois Press, 1991.**

Originally published in 1939, this was the first study of the anti-Chinese movement in the Far West that presaged the anti-Japanese movement around the beginning of the century.

Takaki, Ronald. *Strangers from a Different Shore: A History of Asian Americans.* **New York: Little, Brown, 1989.**

A narrative history of Asian American immigrants, from the Chinese miners in the mid–1800s to the Vietnamese boat people arriving in the 1980s, the book combines historical research and personal anecdotes, with several chapters on Japanese Americans.

Wakatsuki, Yasui. "Japanese Emigration to the United States, 1866–1924." *Perspectives in American History,* **Vol. 12, 1979, pp. 389–516.**

Discusses emigration from Japan to the United States from 1866 to 1924. During these years, thousands of Japanese found work as agricultural workers in the western states.

Wilson, Robert A., and Hosokawa, Bill. *East to America: A History of the Japanese in the United States.* **New York: Quill, 1982.**

Historical account of Japanese life in the United States.

Yanagisako, Sylvia Junko. *Transforming the Past: Tradition and Kinship Among Japanese Americans*. Stanford, CA: Stanford University Press, 1985.

> Describes the changes in family life during Japanese American history.

Fiction

Kanazawa, Tooru J. *Sushi and Sourdough: A Novel*. Seattle: University of Washington Press, 1989.

> A story of the earliest Japanese settlers and adventurers in Alaska during the gold rush at the turn of the century.

Miyamoto, Kazuo. *Hawaii: End of the Rainbow*. Tokyo: Charles E. Tuttle, 1964.

> Epic novel focusing on two generations of a Japanese American family living in Hawaii.

Murayama, Milton. *All I Asking for Is My Body*. Honolulu: University of Hawaii Press, 1988.

> The story of the Oyama family, Murayama's first novel depicts the sugar plantation company towns and villages of Maui.

————. *Five Years on a Rock: A Novel*. Honolulu: University of Hawaii Press, 1994.

> A companion novel to *All I Asking for Is My Body*, it tells the story of Sawa Oyama, a seventeen-year-old picture bride who immigrates to Hawaii in 1915.

Uchida, Yoshiko. *Picture Bride*. New York: Fireside, 1988.

> A novel of a woman who comes to the United States as an *issei* picture bride and ends up being incarcerated in an internment camp during World War II.

Films

Fujikawa. **GPN.**

Explores the lives of Japanese immigrant fishermen in San Pedro, California.

Hito Hata: Raise the Banner. **Visual Communications.**

From the late nineteenth century to the present, this film depicts Japanese immigrants.

Invisible Citizens. **Downtown Community Television.**

Portrays three generations of Japanese Americans.

Picture Bride. **Miramax, 1995.**

A dramatic film about a young picture bride who emigrates to Hawaii to marry a handsome young plantation worker, only to discover that her new life in the United States is like nothing she was promised or ever imagined.

Wataridoro: Birds of Passage. **Amerasia Bookstore.**

Examines the lives of three Japanese American immigrants.

THE *NISEI* AND WORLD WAR II

Nonfiction

Armor, John, and Wright, Peter. *Manzanaar.* **Commentary by John Hersey. Photographs by Ansel Adams. New York: Times Books, 1988.**

A photo essay of life in the internment camp at Manzanaar in California by world-renowned photographer Ansel Adams.

Commission on Wartime Relocation and Internment of Civilians. *Personal Justice Denied,* **2 vols. Washington, DC: U.S. Government Printing Office, 1982.**

Volume 1: The government report on the relocation and internment of Japanese Americans during World War II. Volume 2: The commission's recommendations for compensating survivors.

Crost, Lyn. *Honor by Fire: Japanese Americans at War in Europe and the Pacific*. Novato, CA: Presidio Press, 1994.

By a World War II correspondent who covered the all-*nisei* 100th Battalion and 442nd Combat Team, this is a historical and personal account of those two units in action in Europe, as well as of the *nisei* who served in the Pacific.

Daniels, Roger. *Prisoners Without Trial: Japanese Americans in World War II*. New York: Hill and Wang, 1993.

A summary account of the relocation and internment of Japanese American civilians during World War II and the movement for redress in the 1980s.

Dower, John. *War Without Mercy: Race and Power in the Pacific War*. New York: Pantheon, 1987.

An account of the role of race in the conflict between the United States and Japan during World War II, drawing on popular songs, cartoons, slogans, and propaganda films from both countries.

Duus, Masayo. *Unlikely Liberators: The Men of the 100th and 442nd*. Translated by Peter Duus. Honolulu: University of Hawaii Press, 1983.

The story of the accomplishments of the all-*nisei* 100th Battalion and 442nd Combat Team in World War II, based on official records and nearly 300 interviews with war veterans.

Hosokawa, Bill. *Nisei: The Quiet Americans.*
New York: William Morrow, 1969.

A comprehensive account of the lives of the *nisei*, from the days before World War II up to the late 1960s; its emphasis is on the war years, 1941 to 1945, when the *nisei* came of age.

Irons, Peter. *Justice at War: The Story of the Japanese American Internment Cases.* **New York: Oxford University Press, 1983.**

A behind-the-scenes account of the political and legal battles surrounding the relocation and internment of Japanese Americans during World War II.

Knaefler, Tomi Kaizawa. *Our House Divided: Seven Japanese American Families in World War II.* **Honolulu: University of Hawaii Press, 1991.**

Oral histories recounting the experiences of seven Japanese American families during World War II.

Nelson, Douglas W. *Heart Mountain: The History of an American Concentration Camp.* **Madison, WI: State Historical Society of Wisconsin, 1976.**

A study of the Heart Mountain Relocation Center in Wyoming, where Japanese Americans were interned during World War II.

Shirey, Orville C. *Americans: The Story of the 442nd Combat Team.* **Washington, DC: Infantry Journal Press, 1946.**

The official unit history of the 442nd and 100th Battalion in World War II, with complete lists of the men who served in those units.

Smith, Page. *Democracy on Trial: The Japanese-American Evacuation and Relocation in World War II.* **New York: Simon & Schuster, 1995.**

A comprehensive history of the internment of Japanese

Americans during World War II, based on interviews with former internees and archival research.

Sone, Monica. *Nisei Daughter*. Boston: Little, Brown, 1953.

An autobiographical account of a second-generation Japanese American childhood.

TenBroek, Jacobus, et al. *Prejudice, War and the Constitution: Causes and Consequences of the Evacuation of the Japanese Americans in World War II*. Berkeley and Los Angeles: University of California Press, 1954.

Examines events leading up to and the aftermath of the internment of Japanese Americans during World War II.

Thomas, Dorothy S.; Kikuchi, Charles; and Sakoda, James. *The Salvage*. Berkeley and Los Angeles: University of California Press, 1949.

Concerns the resettlement of Japanese Americans following internment during World War II. Even though the internment was officially over in 1944, thousands of Japanese Americans remained in the camps because they had nowhere to go.

Weglyn, Michi. *Years of Infamy: The Untold Story of America's Concentration Camps*. New York: William Morrow, 1976.

One of the first comprehensive accounts of the internment of Japanese Americans during World War II.

Fiction
Ehrlich, Gretel. *Heart Mountain*. New York: Penguin, 1989.

A love story set in the Heart Mountain Relocation Center in Wyoming, where Japanese Americans were interned during World War II.

Guterson, David. *Snow Falling on Cedars*. **New York: Harcourt Brace, 1994.**

A novel set on Bainbridge Island, Washington, immediately after World War II, about a Japanese American man accused of murder.

Kogawa, Joy. *Itsuka*. **New York: Anchor Books, 1994.**

Set in Canada in the years after World War II, it tells of Japanese Canadians who were forced to relocate during the war and their efforts to obtain compensation from the government.

———. *Obasan*. **New York: Anchor, 1994.**

This novel about Japanese Canadians who were relocated and interned during World War II received the American Book Award.

Mori, Toshio. *Yokohama, California: Stories*. **Seattle: University of Washington Press, 1985.**

Features an introduction by William Saroyan and a new introduction by Lawson Fusao Inada. Orginally published in 1949. Twenty-two stories set in the fictional Japanese American community of Yokohama, California, in the 1930s and 1940s.

Okada, John. *No-No Boy*. **Seattle: University of Washington Press, 1979.**

Introduction by Lawson Fusao Inada. Afterword by Frank Chin. This novel tells of a *nisei* held in an internment camp who refuses to swear allegiance to the United States or serve in the military. After the war he is shunned by other Japanese Americans for the choices he made.

Yamauchi, Wakako. *Songs My Mother Taught Me*. **New York: Feminist Press, 1994.**

A collection of stories and plays about the lives of *issei* and *nisei,* from World War II and its aftermath. Also included are personal recollections about the author's own experiences.

Poetry

Inada, Lawson Fusao. *Before the War: Poems as They Happened.* New York: William Morrow, 1971.

A collection of poems by a *sansei* (third-generation) Japanese American writer who grew up in an internment camp during World War II. A number of the poems describe his experiences in the camps.

————. *Legends from the Camp.* Minneapolis: Coffee House, 1993.

A collection of fifty poems ranging from Inada's experiences in camp to the years after the war.

Films

***Color of Honor: The Japanese American Soldier in World War II.* Vox Productions.**

Features Japanese American graduates of the Military Intelligence Service Language School who worked during World War II as translators and interrogators in the Asian/Pacific theater.

***Come See the Paradise.* UCLA Film TV, 1990.**

A story of a Japanese American family torn apart by the relocation and internment during World War II.

***Days of Waiting.* National Asian American Telecommunications Association.**

Examines the relationship between a European American wife and her husband, a Japanese American internee.

Farewell to Manzanaar.

A TV movie based on the book by Jeanne Wakatsuki

Houston and James D. Houston.

From Hawaii to the Holocaust: A Shared Moment in History.

A documentary on a little-known episode in the history of World War II: the role of *nisei* soldiers from the 100th/442nd Combat Team in the liberation of the concentration camp at Dachau. (To order VHS, write or call Direct Cinema Limited, P.O. Box 10003, Santa Monica, CA 90410, telephone: 800-525-0000; fax: 310-396-3233).

Nisei Soldier: Standard Bearer for an Exiled People. **Vox Productions, 1983.**

Focuses on the 442nd Regimental Combat Team's Japanese American soldiers. The 442nd was the most decorated unit of its size during World War II. Check with your library or media center for a copy of this documentary. Or contact the distributor, Vox Productions, at 2335 Jones Street, San Francisco, CA 94133.

Meeting at Tule Lake. **Tule Lake Committee, 1994.**

A documentary about the Tule Lake Detention Camp and Segregation Center, the internment camp where Japanese Americans who were considered "subversive" or "disloyal" were held. The army guarded the camp with tanks and enforced strict regulations. Check your library media center.

Survivors.

A documentary about Japanese Americans who were caught in the atomic bombings of Hiroshima and Nagasaki in August 1945. (To order or rent, contact The Video Project, 5332 College Avenue, Suite 101, Oakland, CA 94618, telephone: 800-475-2638; fax: 510-655-9115.)

Unfinished Business: The Japanese American Internment Cases. National Asian American Telecommunications Association.

Delves into cases of Japanese American internment. Former president Ronald Reagan, on August 10, 1988, signed into law an entitlement program to provide financial compensation to former internees.

Chapter 2
Beginning Your Genealogical Search

Tools

Like any project, a genealogical search requires tools. The tools you will need are:

- File cabinets, crates, or boxes. For old documents, artifacts. Many of the records you uncover—birth certificates, immigration records, etc.—are available only in photocopy form and will need to be stored.
- Photo album. Because you may uncover photos that are old and decaying, use albums that have protective covering on each page.
- File folders. You will need to organize each household or family group into separate folders. Hanging file folders are good to use with file crates and file boxes.
- Looseleaf notebooks. Use one for note-taking, a second for the family history book itself.[1]
- Pedigree chart, or family tree. A chart that lists each generation of a family. You can create a chart or buy a preprinted chart from a bookstore. If you are using a computer, software programs for creating a family tree are available on the market.
- Family group sheets. Worksheets for recording information about family groups or households.
- Tape recorder or camcorder. Optional, for recording interviews. Be sure to ask an interviewee for permis-

---

[1] If you choose to work with a computer, it is probably a good idea to print out files and keep hard copies in a looseleaf binder.

sion to record his or her interview beforehand. (See chapter 4 on "Oral History".)

Getting Started

A story from India tells of a man walking down a street at night and coming across an old woman standing under a street lamp. She is scanning the ground for something. He stops and asks: "Did you lose something?" "A key," she mutters in response. "I lost it somewhere in my house." "But why are you looking out here, then?" the man asks, puzzled. "Ah, the light's much better out here than in my house," she replies.[2]

The story may be silly, but it is instructive. When you begin a genealogical search, it is best to start within the family. Complete a pedigree chart for yourself or the family member closest to you. The chart should include as much of the following information as applies: birth date and birthplace of subject; parents' and grandparents' names, birthplaces, birth dates, places and dates of marriage; names, birth dates, and places of other children, etc.

Gather the most basic information. It should fall into four categories: names; dates; places; relationships. According to the National Archives guide *Using Records in the National Archives for Genealogical Research*: "People can be identified in records by their names, by the dates of events in their lives (birth, marriage, death), by the places where they lived, and by their relationships to others."

When you fill out a family pedigree chart, list each person by surname (or last name), first name, middle name, capitalizing the entire surname. List dates by day, month, year: for example, 7 December 1941. For places, go from small (e.g., towns) to big (e.g., states): for example, Jersey City, Hudson County, New Jersey. These ways of listing will help when the search takes you to libraries and public archives.

The pedigree chart is flexible; it can extend as far back in

---

[2] Ramanujan, *Folktales from India*, p. xiv.

Pedigree Chart

Name of Compiler _____

Address _____

City, State _____

Date _____

Person No.1 on this chart is the same person as No.____on chart No.____.

Chart No.____

b. Date of Birth
p.b. Place of Birth
m. Date of Marriage
d. Date of Death
p.d. Place of Death

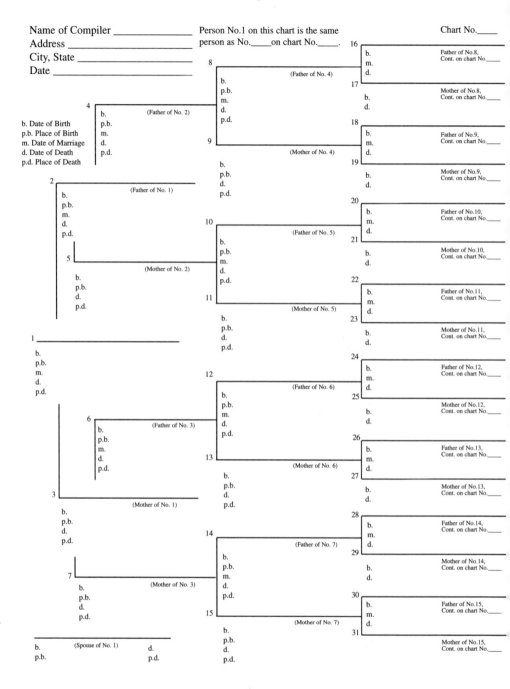

8 (Father of No. 4)

4 (Father of No. 2)
b.
p.b.
m.
d.
p.d.

9 (Mother of No. 4)

2 (Father of No. 1)
b.
p.b.
m.
d.
p.d.

10 (Father of No. 5)

5 (Mother of No. 2)
b.
p.b.
d.
p.d.

11 (Mother of No. 5)

1 _____
b.
p.b.
m.
d.
p.d.

12 (Father of No. 6)

6 (Father of No. 3)
b.
p.b.
m.
d.
p.d.

13 (Mother of No. 6)

3 (Mother of No. 1)
b.
p.b.
d.
p.d.

14 (Father of No. 7)

7 (Mother of No. 3)
b.
p.b.
d.
p.d.

15 (Mother of No. 7)

8
b.
p.b.
m.
d.
p.d.

9
b.
p.b.
d.
p.d.

10
b.
p.b.
m.
d.
p.d.

11
b.
p.b.
d.
p.d.

12
b.
p.b.
m.
d.
p.d.

13
b.
p.b.
d.
p.d.

14
b.
p.b.
m.
d.
p.d.

15
b.
p.b.
d.
p.d.

16
b.
m.
d.
Father of No.8,
Cont. on chart No.____

17
b.
d.
Mother of No.8,
Cont. on chart No.____

18
b.
m.
d.
Father of No.9,
Cont. on chart No.____

19
b.
d.
Mother of No.9,
Cont. on chart No.____

20
b.
m.
d.
Father of No.10,
Cont. on chart No.____

21
b.
d.
Mother of No.10,
Cont. on chart No.____

22
b.
m.
d.
Father of No.11,
Cont. on chart No.____

23
b.
d.
Mother of No.11,
Cont. on chart No.____

24
b.
m.
d.
Father of No.12,
Cont. on chart No.____

25
b.
d.
Mother of No.12,
Cont. on chart No.____

26
b.
m.
d.
Father of No.13,
Cont. on chart No.____

27
b.
d.
Mother of No.13,
Cont. on chart No.____

28
b.
m.
d.
Father of No.14,
Cont. on chart No.____

29
b.
d.
Mother of No.14,
Cont. on chart No.____

30
b.
m.
d.
Father of No.15,
Cont. on chart No.____

31
b.
d.
Mother of No.15,
Cont. on chart No.____

(Spouse of No. 1)
b.
p.b.
d.
p.d.

time as you want by simply adding more pages. It is important to number each person on the charts, so that you can continue onto additional pages. For instance, on the charts on pp. 78 and 80, the subject's paternal grandfather is number 4. If you wanted to continue to trace his ancestors, you would start a new chart, numbered 4. He would go in the first slot, with his father and mother on each side, and their parents after them.

How Far to Go?

With basic information about the most immediate ancestors, you can decide how far to search. If you stick to direct ancestors (parents and grandparents), you can fill out a pedigree chart with at least seven entries; more if there are stepparents or stepgrandparents. If you go two generations further, to great-great-grandparents, there will be at least thirty entries on the family tree; two more generations, to great-great-great-great-grandparents, at least 126. Tracing a contemporary Japanese American family back to its Japanese roots will probably require going back at least three generations.

You might want to trace a family back two or three centuries; or you might just want to learn about the generation that grew up during World War II. Your original plan may change after you get started. You might set out to create an elaborate family tree, only to discover a little-known ancestor whose story captures the imagination. Or you could be looking up a female family member's maiden name, only to discover a well-known historical figure in the family. Either way, you should follow your curiosity.

Interviewing Persons to Complete Pedigree Charts and Family Group Sheets

Family members, friends, old neighbors, godparents, colleagues, teachers—any of these people can provide valuable information. Create a questionnaire. If you interview a person face to face, you can use the questionnaire as a guide. If a person lives far away, or does not have time for a live

FAMILY GROUP WORK SHEET #_____

HUSBAND, Name: WIFE, Name:

Birth:	Place:
Death:	Place:
Burial:	Place:
Father:	
Mother:	
Occupation:	
Notes:	

Birth:	Place:
Death:	Place:
Burial:	Place:
Father:	
Mother:	
Occupation:	
Notes:	

Name	Date & Place of Birth	Date & Place of Marriage	Date & Place of Death	Married to	Date & Place of Birth	Death

interview, you can simply mail or fax a copy and ask him or her to complete it.

Questions to ask about a family member might include: Full name? Nicknames? Birth date and birthplace? Wedding date and place (if applicable)? If deceased, date of death? Place of burial?

This information is for the pedigree chart. Information for the family group sheets might include: What jobs have the various family members held? Where did they go to school? Did they serve in the military? Are/were they involved in their communities? What are/were their hobbies, interests? Do/did they have any religious affiliation? Use this information to start a family group sheet about each branch of a family. Put each family group's sheet into a separate file folder.

Other useful questions might be: Is there a family plot or cemetery? Where? Are there any famous people in the family? Has anything been written about him/her/them? Has anyone else traced the family's history? Does anyone in the family own scrapbooks, old photos, letters, diaries, journals, the family Bible, etc.? Record this information in your notebook. It may give you ideas about where to look for missing information in the future.

Live interviews should be short: no more than one hour at a time. If more time is needed, arrange to meet again. Interviews are best done in private. Speak clearly, and get to the point. A rule of thumb for journalists is the "five Ws": who, what, where, when, why (and sometimes how). Each question should begin with one of the five Ws. Be a good listener. (See chapter 4 on "Oral History.")

After the interview, transcribe (or type up) the interview and send a copy of it to the interviewee, or informant, for his or her corrections. You will find that people will often add information that occurred to them afterward. Be sure to thank each person in writing and let him or her know that the completed family history will be available for the asking.

If you interview persons by mail or fax, send a questionnaire form along with a blank pedigree chart and a cover letter. The letter should announce what you are doing and politely ask for help; it should end by thanking the person in advance. If writing to a stranger, you will have to introduce yourself. You will also want to enclose copies of pedigree charts and family group sheets you have already completed, to let the informant know what you have already accomplished.

The cover letter is very important. A polite, straight-forward, well-written letter will improve your chances of getting the information you need. A badly written or rude letter will very likely be thrown in the trash, along with the questionnaire and charts. See the example below.

Sample Cover Letter for Interviewing People by Mail

Dear _____ :

I am trying to gather information in order to put together a history of the _____ family. I would be grateful if you could find the time to fill in the blank pedigree chart and questionnaire enclosed. Please fill in as much information as you can. I have also enclosed copies of what I have done so far. (If you find any mistakes, please let me know.) When you have finished with these, please return them in the stamped, self-addressed envelope enclosed.

It would be a great help, too, if you could tell me who else in the _____ family might have information about ancestors, or if you have any information or documents that I might copy and return. I want to record and preserve the _____ family's history as accurately and completely as possible.

When I have completed my research, I will be happy to share the results with you. Please let me know if you are interested in receiving a copy of my final pedigree chart. Thank you so much for your time and help.

Sincerely yours,

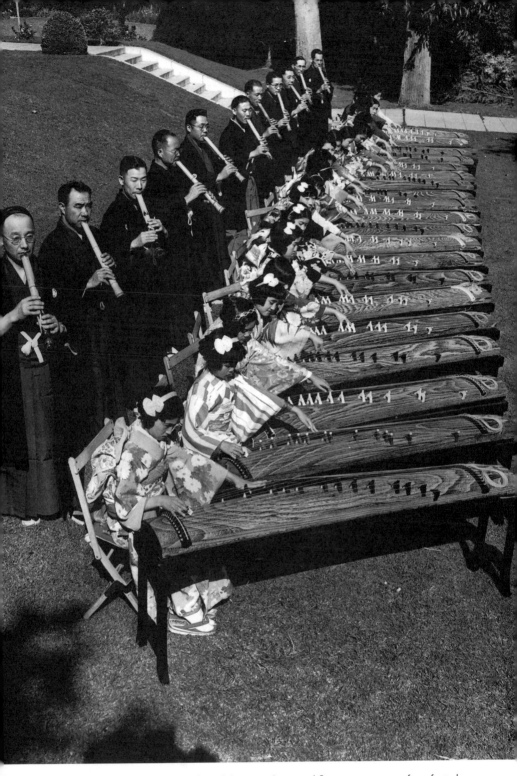

Japanese musicians practice on traditional Japanese harps and flutes in preparation for a festival in Los Angeles in 1937. Musical instruments may be among the heirlooms in your own family.

Keep copies or a list of the requests sent out to avoid duplicate letters. Along with the chart, questionnaire, and letter, enclose a self-addressed envelope with correct postage.

Artifacts and Records

The next step is searching for family artifacts and records. You can learn a lot from birth certificates, school records, church records, marriage licenses, driver's licenses, passports, as well as mementos such as diaries, journals, letters, birth announcements, wedding announcements, obituaries, old report cards, baptismal certificates, baby books, awards, greeting cards, etc. Find out if the family possesses a family Bible where births, deaths, marriages, and other such information is usually recorded.

Stored objects can also reveal much about a Japanese American family history. A copy of a War Relocation Authority pamphlet "Questions and Answers for Evacuees" from 1942 tells you that a family member might have been interned in a relocation center during World War II. Small round metal badges with numbers could be identification tags (*bangō*) from a Hawaiian plantation. You might guess, then, that somebody in the family worked on a sugarcane plantation in Hawaii. Therefore it is very likely he or she came from southern Honshu or Kyushu island in Japan, as did the majority of immigrants to Hawaii.

Objects from Japan such as clothing can give clues to when an immigrant arrived, in the Meiji era (before 1912), the Taisho era (1912 to 1926), or the Showa era (after 1926). They can also tell what region of Japan that person came from. For instance, a kimono made from banana fiber, rather than silk or cotton, is unusual; most likely it came from the island of Okinawa.

Old artifacts can also be instructive to anyone interested in Japanese life and culture. An old notebook from a Japanese school might be filled with Japanese characters. You might find old carp flags used to celebrate *Tango no sekku* (Boys' Day, May 5) or the porcelain dolls, or *ningyo*, which are displayed for *Hinamatsuri* (Girls' Day, March 3). Someone who has paper lanterns for the *O-bon* may be able to tell about the festival for the dead.

Remember that personal records and mementos are private property. Do not go rummaging through anyone's desk drawers, closets, or attic without permission. Do not take anything unless it is offered. If you are lent or given an object, make sure it is stored properly. Do not dump a hundred-year-old family relic in the corner of a closet or under a bed. Records and documents should be photocopied, if possible, and returned right away. Never misuse other people's mementos and keepsakes.

Old Photographs

Old photographs are our most immediate link to the past; often they are the last remnant of earlier generations. They can tell how elders looked when they were young, what their homes were like, or other important biographical facts. A portrait of a woman in a wedding kimono might have been an exchange photo (*kokan shashin*), the kind used in picture bride marriages. Photos can also be used to identify people, places, and times. How a picture was taken, who took it, and who is in the picture—these are important questions to keep in mind.

Old photographs should be filed for easy identification and access. For photo albums, the simplest method is to number them Album 1, Album 2, etc. Then number each photograph in each album: for example, Album 1:1 (photo 1 in Album 1), Album 1:2 (photo 2 in Album 1), Album 2:1 (photo 1 in Album 2), and so on. Then, keep a card file (either index cards or using Card File ™ software) with a separate card for each photo, listing the photo number and recording any information about the picture: subject(s), where it was taken, when, by whom. For loose photographs, start a separate album and assign it and the photos in it their own numbers.

Sometimes you will find all the information you need written on the backs of photographs. For example, a picture might have the legend: "Me and my parents, Coney Island,

Family photographs are not only valuable keepsakes but can also be useful genealogical tools for the purpose of identifying individuals and events.

New York, 10/21/63." Then all you have to do is identify
the child in the picture. Or an elementary school class portrait may include a signboard with the name of the school,
the teacher's name, and the year.

Not all of the photos will be so obvious, however. Often
you have to deduce information, like a detective, from clues
in the picture itself. Landmarks can tell where a photo was
taken; the make of cars can tell when; photographers' stamps
can tell who took it; clothing can identify a subject.

Say you find an old group portrait of people at a wedding.
You do not recognize the bride and groom. Only the name
and address of a photo studio is stamped on back. By check-
ing the family group charts, you might be able to match the
town or city where the studio is located to the place where
these people got married. Then you discover that everyone
in the family was married in the same church. What is more,
they all used the same photographer.

You will have to look for clues in the picture itself. You
see that the groom has wavy hair, while the bride's hair is
short and kinky. In the background are silver streamers; the
floor is spangled with light reflecting off a revolving ball.
Two of the men in the group are wearing shiny white suits
that are too tight and black shirts half-buttoned. On the far
right is a man dressed in a lime-green leisure suit. From
these details you can guess that the picture was probably
taken in the late 1970s. By cross-checking family group
charts and asking family members, you will have a good
chance of identifying the mystery couple.

Family Reunions

One way to share and gather information about your family
is to organize a family reunion. Begin by asking immediate
family members if they would be interested in attending or
possibly even helping you plan a reunion. If you get a
number of positive responses, you can begin to plan the
occasion by gathering addresses of your relatives.

Next, compile a form letter, stating your intentions about
having a reunion and mail it to all of your relatives,

enclosing the list of people that you are contacting. In your letter inquire about obtaining more names and addresses of family members.

As you are building a list of people to invite, choose a date—far enough in advance so vacation time can be allocated—and place to have the reunion. Mail notices to everyone and advertise the reunion in newspapers and genealogical publications. Unless you have the money to spend, you may want to charge a fee or ask for donations. Most people won't mind paying a nominal fee in order to see family members that they may have never met before.

Activities may include storytelling—which you will want to tape record, sharing and going through photo albums, preparing and sampling traditional Japanese foods, filling out family trees, and more. During the reunion, take many photographs and, if possible, videotape the party. The pictures and videotapes will become part of your family history. With many of your family members present, a reunion can be a perfect opportunity for obtaining more information about your heritage.

Asking for Assistance

When approaching others, keep in mind that not everyone will want to take part. Do not try to twist anyone's arm. No one is obliged to help. In fact, chances are good that a search will come to a grinding halt if you start abusing the goodwill of others. You cannot search a family history without help from that family. But if you ask nicely, stating your intentions clearly and up front, your chances of winning cooperation will be greatly improved.

Your research is off to a good start by now. Remember that your methods should be consistent, but the receipt of information may not occur in the order you look for it. You will invariably come to sticking points, or dead ends, but that doesn't mean the search is over. The more you discover, the greater the number of possible approaches that are opened to you for answers. You will grow better at gene-

A Japanese American Photo Album

Japan is geographically a small country compared to the United States, but its distinctive culture has become a vital part of the American mosaic. Many Japanese American families have lived in the United States for several generations; their ancestors often worked tirelessly in Hawaii's sugarcane fields or on California's farmlands, providing the cheap labor that would develop the growing Western states. When Japan's mountainous landscape and thin soil offered little agricultural land, or when political problems resulted in widespread poverty, Japanese emigrants sought better lives in the United States. More often than not, they met with exploitation, discrimination, and racism.

Yet they worked hard and became a part of the American community. Young Japanese American soldiers fought bravely on the side of the United States in World War II even as their fellow Japanese Americans were held in internment camps because of American suspicions. Today, Japanese Americans have risen to the top of their fields in academia, politics, science, sports, and many other professions. As you research your family's Japanese American history, think about obstacles they may have overcome and the successes they have enjoyed. Look not only at your family's legacy, but at the legacy of all Japanese Americans. You have reasons to feel proud to be Japanese American, a part of one of the cultural groups that have made the United States what it is today.

Tokyo, one of the world's largest and most expensive cities, is a fitting capital for an economically powerful, technologically advanced country such as Japan. The Ginza district, one of Tokyo's most famous neighborhoods, is known for its glamorous shopping boulevards and vibrant nightlife.

While Japan is often portrayed in terms of Tokyo's dense urban spaces and neon lights, another side of Japan is rural and agricultural. Many residents of the countryside continue to do things as they have been done for generations. Above, a Japanese woman washes clothes in a stream beside a thatched-roof water mill.

The Japanese celebrate many festivals throughout the year. *Shichi-Go-San* is an annual event that honors young girls and boys and ushers them into society. Girls participate in the event when they are between five and seven years old; boys, when they are between three and five. On that day, children dress in their best clothes and visit a shrine.

Tanabata Matsuri, the Star Festival, originated in the city of Hiratsuka, Japan, thirty-five miles south of Tokyo. The festival is an opportunity to pray for a good harvest and to present offerings of fruit to the stars. Above, a street in Hiratsuka is colorfully decorated for the five-day ceremony.

Cherry blossoms, one of Japan's best-loved flowers, frame a view of the Hieram Shrine in Kyoto, Japan.

Japanese American women take part in a cherry-blossom festival in San Francisco.

An elderly mourner holds a Japanese flag during the funeral procession of Emperor Hirohito, who died in 1989. Japan is a constitutional monarchy, with both a hereditary emperor and a parliamentary system of government. The emperor's function is largely ceremonial. Emperor Hirohito was succeeded by his son, Akihito.

Along with Buddhism, Shintoism is one of Japan's major religions. Many Buddhists practice Shintoism as well; it was the state religion of Japan until the end of World War II. This small Shinto shrine in the rice paddies south of Tokyo is believed to ensure a bountiful yield because it honors the God of Good Harvest.

Signs of tradition endure in contemporary Japan. Hideo Matsutani, a retired police officer and kite-maker, tests the strings on a huge rice-paper kite. Kite-making is a traditional Japanese art.

Young Japanese in kimonos visit a shrine to offer New Year's prayers.

Japanese Americans continue to express their Japanese heritage through cultural festivals and the endurance of Japanese American communities. Above, Japanese Americans turn out in traditional clothing at a multicultural festival in New York City.

San Francisco was an important port of entry for the first Japanese immigrants. Many settled there, and in the early 1900s the city became the site of the Japanese Association of America headquarters. San Francisco still has a strong Japanese American community, symbolized by its Japantown. Above, a merchant awaits customers in his Japantown store.

Japanese gardens are favorite sites for tranquility and relaxation in cities throughout the United States. Above, a woman in traditional attire strolls in the Japanese Garden in San Jose, California.

One-hundred-year-old Sugi Kiriyama, a resident of Los Angeles, was one of the first recipients of $20,000 in reparations paid to Japanese Americans who were interned during World War II. The payment of reparations, which began in 1990, was meant to compensate Japanese Americans for the homes, possessions, and jobs they lost during the internment. The sum could not, of course, erase the suffering experienced by Japanese Americans during this dark hour of American history.

Japanese American figure skater Kristi Yamaguchi won a gold medal in women's figure skating in the 1992 Winter Olympics in Albertville, France. She was joined on the podium by the silver medalist, Midori Ito, of Japan, and fellow American and bronze-medal winner Nancy Kerrigan.

alogy the more you work at it. You will learn how to use resources to their maximum benefit and become more adept at learning how to find what you need. Be persistent; think, learn, and work hard.

Resources

GENEALOGY BASICS

Alessi, Jean, and Miller, Jan. *Once Upon a Memory: Your Family Tales and Treasures.* White Hall, VA: Betterway Publications, 1987.

A guide to tracing your family history by interviewing family members and examining household items, photos, personal records. Bibliography, illustrations, index.

Allen, Desmond Walls, and Billingsley, Carolyn Earle. *Beginner's Guide to Family History Research.* Bountiful, UT: American Genealogical Lending Library, 1991.

A step-by-step guide to starting a family history search, it includes sample charts, illustrations, appendixes.

American Genealogy: A Basic Course. National Genealogical Society, 4527 17th Street North, Arlington, VA 22207-2363.

A home-study program on organizing a family history search using written and video material.

Ashton, Rick J., and Sinko, Peggy Tuck. *The Genealogy Beginner's Manual.* Chicago: Newberry Library, 1977.

An introduction to genealogical research.

Brown, Norman. *The Trace Your Own Roots Workbook.* New York: Grosset & Dunlap, 1978.

An instruction guide on researching and writing a family history.

Cooper, Kay. *Where Did You Get Those Eyes: A Guide to Discovering Your Family History.* **New York: Walker & Co., 1988.**

A step-by-step guide to creating a family tree, from interviewing parents and relatives to conducting research in a genealogical library. Reprinted as *Discover It Yourself: Where Did You Get Those Eyes?* (Avon, 1993.)

Davies, Thomas L. *Shoots: A Guide to Your Family's Photographic Heritage.* **Danbury, NH: Addison House, 1987.**

A handbook to preserving and restoring old photographs, as well as dating and identifying them.

Dollarhide, William. *Managing a Genealogical Project: A Complete Manual for the Management and Organization of Genealogical Materials.* **Baltimore: Genealogical Publishing, 1988.**

A guide to organizing family history materials and documentation by the designer of the computer software Everyone's Family Tree (see below).

Draznin, Yaffa. *The Family Historian's Handbook.* **New York: Jove/HBJ, 1978.**

A complete how-to guide for tracing family histories of all ethnic backgrounds.

Earnest, Russell D. *Grandma's Attic: Making Heirlooms Part of Your Family History.* **Albuquerque, NM: R. D. Earnest Assoc., 1991.**

This book will help you to determine the significance of items you may find in the course of talking to relatives and rummaging through family keepsakes. The author provides advice on how to incorporate these items into a family history.

Everton's Genealogical Helper
3223 South Main Street
Nibley, UT 84321

Bimonthly publication, available at many libraries.

Frish-Ripley, Karen. *Unlocking Secrets in Old Photos.* **Salt Lake City: Ancestry Inc., 1991.**

A step-by-step guide to using photos to create or fill in a family tree. It includes instructions on how to date photos, recognize photo types, identify faces in pictures, restore old photos, and find photos. Bibliography, index.

Getting Started: Beginning Your Genealogical Research in the National Archives. **Washington, DC: General Services Administration, 1983.**

A guide to using census records, military service and pension records, and passenger arrival and naturalization records in a genealogical search.

A Handy Book for Genealogists. **Logan, UT: Everton, 1989.**

A useful introduction to family history.

Helmbold, F. Wilbur. *Tracing Your Ancestry: Step-by-Step Guide to Researching Your Family History.* **Birmingham, AL: Oxmoor House, 1978.**

A basic instructive guide to using genealogical sources to trace a family history.

Heritage Quest. **American Genealogical Lending Library.**

A bimonthly magazine that features classified ads placed by people offering or seeking information and services. It also contains articles on topics such as computer software and adoption searches.

Hibberts, Joyce Whaler, and Saffell, Kathleen Kirkpatrick. *A Primer in Beginning Genealogy.* **Ridgecrest, CA: Saffell's Naturally, 1989.**

A guide to organizing your search, sources, and finding official documents, including federal records.

Hilton, Suzanne. *Who Do You Think You Are? Digging for Your Family Roots.* **Philadelphia, PA: Westminster Press, 1976.**

A step-by-step guide on how to trace your ancestors and construct a family tree. Illustrations.

Immigrant Genealogical Society Newsletter
P.O. Box 7369
Burbank, CA 91510-7369

Monthly newsletter available also in some libraries.

Kikumura, Akemi. *Issei Pioneers: Hawaii and the Mainland, 1885 to 1924.* **Los Angeles: Japanese American National Museum, 1992.**

Contains pictures of the clothing, homes, and personal belongings of the *issei,* also useful in identifying old objects and their use by an immigrant ancestor.

Lichtman, Allan J. *Your Family History.* **New York: Vintage, 1978.**

A guide to creating a personal family history using personal records, interviews, and public records. It includes sample family trees, personal information charts, and suggested questions for oral history interviews. Bibliography, illustrations, index.

Meyer, Mary K. *Meyer's Directory of Genealogical Societies in the USA and Canada.* **Mt. Airy, MD: Mary K. Meyer, 1988.**

A listing of organizations active in genealogical searches; this book may tell you of an organization that can help your own search.

Parker, Kenneth B. *Find Your Roots: A Beginner's Kit for Tracing Your Family Tree.* **Southfield, MI: Lezell-Brasch Associates, 1977.**

This guide for beginners in genealogical research includes sample ancestry charts and family group sheets.

Schreiner-Yantis, Netti.

Designer of widely used family group sheets, pedigree charts, and other forms, which you can buy. For price list, write GBIP, 6818 Lois Drive, Springfield, VA 22150.

———. *Genealogical and Local History Books in Print*, 3 vols, 4th ed. Springfield, VA: Schreiner-Yantis, 1990.

Check one of these volumes for hard-to-find family history manuscripts as well as information on genealogical publications, supplies, and services.

Stryker-Rodda, Harriet. *How to Climb Your Family Tree: A Genealogy for Beginners*. Philadelphia: Lippincott, 1977.

An introduction to the basics of genealogical research.

Time-Life Books. *Caring for Photographs*. New York: Time-Life Books, 1973.

A guide to displaying, storing, and restoring old photos and prints.

Weinstein, Robert A., and Booth, Larry. *Collection, Use and Care of Historical Photographs*. Nashville, TN: American Association for State and Local History, 1977.

A history of photographic methods from 1839 to the present and a guide for treating and preserving old photos.

Westin, Jeane Eddy. *Finding Your Roots: How Every American Can Trace His Ancestors—At Home and Abroad*. New York: Ballantine, 1977.

A guide to creating a family tree, finding lost ancestors, and writing your family history. Bibliography, appendixes.

COMPUTER SOFTWARE

American Genealogical Lending Library
Holdings include electronic databases that can be accessed by telephone, censuses on CD-ROM, and marriage records on disk.

593 West 100
North Bountiful, UT 84010
801-298-5446

Biography Maker
A software program designed for writing a family history. For MS-DOS computers.

Banner Blue Software
P.O. Box 7865
Fremont, CA 94537
510-795-4490

Everyone's Family Tree
User-friendly software designed for beginners. It features an on-screen help manual and automatic name indexing.

Dollarhide Systems
203 Holly Street
Bellingham, WA 28225
206-671-3808

Family Roots and Lineage
Basic family history programs with chart-making and indexing capabilities. Lineage is a lower-priced version of Family Roots.

Quinsept, Inc.
P.O. Box 216
Lexington, MA 02173
800-637-ROOT

Genealogical Computing
This quarterly magazine publishes a directory of genealogical software once a year.

Ancestry Incorporated
440 South 400 West, Building D
Salt Lake City, UT 84104
800-531-1790

Generations Library
A database manager for storing information; it does not have graphics capabilities for producing charts or indexing.

Interlock Software Systems
P.O. Box 130953
Houston, TX 77219
713-680-8576

KinWrite and KinPublish
KinWrite is a basic family history program, with graphics that can reproduce photos with a scanner. KinPublish is a desktop publisher that produces professional-quality text and graphics.

LDB Association, Inc.
Dept. Q Box 20837
Wichita, KS 67208-6837
316-683-6200

Personal Ancestral File
Perhaps the best-known software for genealogical research.

Ancestral File Operations Unit
50 East North Temple Street
Salt Lake City, UT 84150
801-240-2584

Roots IV
Software that allows flexible entries for nontraditional family histories.

Commsoft, Inc.
7795 Bell Road
P.O. Box 310
Windsor, CA 95495-0130

GENEALOGY ON THE INTERNET

If you have a modem and access to the Internet, you have an enormous wealth of genealogical materials at your fingertips. The speed of on-line communication has become a boon for genealogical researchers who want to access archives and libraries or who want to "talk" to each other through e-mail or discussion groups. The following are some useful Internet addresses for genealogists:

Genealogy Online

    http://genealogy.org

National Genealogical Society

    http://genealogy.org/NGS

U.S. Bureau of the Census Home Page

    http://www.census.gov
    ftp://gateway.census.gov

U.S. National Archives

    gopher://gopher.nara.gov
    http://www.nara.gov

Chapter 3
Using Outside Sources

Local Libraries and Records

The library in the hometown of the family you are researching should have at least one local history, which might include references to ancestors. Or the library may even have a
previous family history. Other sources that can help are
newspapers, school yearbooks, even old telephone directories. And of course most, if not all, of the works listed in this
book can be found in libraries.

If unfamiliar with a library, ask the librarian for directions,
a map, or even a quick tour. If you say you are conducting
genealogical research, the librarian should be able to direct
you to specific sources that can help you.

Old newspapers can be especially useful. Obituaries are
helpful because they give short biographies. So do wedding
announcements, career milestones, and graduation notices.
Some newspapers have indexes of names, listed by year.
Otherwise you need to know the approximate date or at least
the month and year of the item you want.

In cities and communities with large Japanese American
populations, you can find newspapers published exclusively
by and for the Japanese American community. Some, such
as the *Hawaii Shimpo*, are written in Japanese. Others, such
as the Los Angeles *Rafu Shimpo*, have both Japanese and
English sections. Others, such as the *Japanese American
Courier* of Seattle, are written in English.[1]

These newspapers covered life events of local Japanese
Americans: deaths, funerals, births, marriages, anniversaries,

---

[1] For a partial list of Japanese American newspapers listed by city, see
Gubler, pp. 118–121.

Ship passenger lists, which can be obtained from LDS Family History Centers, may provide valuable clues about your ancestors' date of arrival and point of origin. These Japanese immigrants arrived in the United States on the liner *Shinyu Maru,* which docked in San Francisco in 1920.

and new arrivals. They are good places to search for information about the family's Japanese origins—the name of the *issei* (first-generation) ancestor, his or her hometown, and names of relatives. Most of these newspapers were written either partly or entirely in Japanese.

If researching persons from other towns and states, you can write to the local library in their hometown. Be specific about what you are looking for. You might write something like:

> I am researching [NAME], who lived in [CITY] from 1909 to 1941. Can you tell me if his name appears in any local history or family genealogy in your collection? Also, could you direct me to any local genealogical, historical, or Japanese American ethnic organizations that I might consult for my research?

Be sure to include a self-addressed, stamped envelope for a reply, and thank the librarian in advance. The library may charge you a small fee for its services, including photocopying.

Genealogical Associations and Publications, Historical Societies

Throughout the country, numerous genealogical associations and private libraries are devoted to tracing family histories. The largest such institution in the world is the Family History Library of the LDS Church (The Church of Jesus Christ of Latter-day Saints) in Salt Lake City, Utah. It holds information on roughly 2 billion people: census records, land grants, deeds, marriage records, wills, naturalization records, passenger ship lists, and more. From transcribing vital records from all over the world, LDS has developed an International Genealogy Index (IGI) that contains statistics on more than 150 million persons who died between 1500 and 1875. The LDS also maintains a Family Registry so that people who are researching the same name can have access to each other and share information.

There are many LDS Family History Centers scattered across the country. To find one near you, look in the telephone book or write to the LDS Family History Library, 35 North West Temple Street, Salt Lake City, UT 84150. Also, public libraries in large cities, such as the New York Public Library and the Los Angeles Public Library, have extensive genealogical collections.

There are also genealogical societies and organizations that help family historians with their searches. One is the National Genealogical Society, 4527 17th Street North, Arlington, VA 22207-2363; 703-525-0050, which sells research aids, preprinted family group sheets and pedigree charts, and instructional books. It also publishes a quarterly magazine, the *National Genealogical Society Quarterly*, and a newsletter for family researchers, the *NGS Newsletter*.

Some historical organizations that may be especially helpful to the research of a Japanese American family are:

National Japanese American Historical Society
1855 Folsom Street, Suite 161
San Francisco, CA 94103-4232
415-431-5007 / fax: 415-431-0311

Japanese American National Museum
369 East First Street
Los Angeles, CA 90012
213-625-0414 / fax: 213-625-1770

You can also try the Japanese American Citizens League, which has 115 chapters throughout the United States and in Japan. The original chapter is at:

1765 Sutter Street
San Francisco, CA 94115
415-921-5225

On the East Coast, contact the New York office at:

726 Broadway
New York, NY 10013
212-921-5768

These organizations may be able to answer some of your questions about Japanese American history, or direct you to likely sources of information.

Public Archives, Government Records

Birth certificates, death certificates, and marriage licenses are usually kept in county and state offices. The U.S. Government Printing Office publishes a leaflet, *Where to Write for Vital Records: Births, Deaths, Marriages, and Divorces*, which tells how to obtain these records. To order this leaflet write to the Superintendent of Documents, U.S. Government Printing Office, Washington, DC 20402. Churches also keep records of baptisms and marriages. You can write or call the local diocese or parish of the subject's church to find out where to write for the necessary records.

In addition to these vital records, property deeds are kept in local and county courthouses and are available on request. Remember, though, that most *issei* were barred from owning land in the 1920s. Many of them incorporated their farms under false names or signed deeds in their children's names, which may complicate a search.

For *issei* two or three generations removed, you might do better searching in state archives and the National Archives. The records they keep—including census records, naturalization records, and passenger lists for steamships—can help fill in the details of an *issei*'s arrival in America.

You can request a search for that information from the Immigration and Naturalization Service (INS), a branch of the Department of Justice. You will have to fill out Form G-641, "Application for Verification from Immigration and Naturalization Records" and pay a fee. These forms are available at INS offices in major cities. Check your local telephone directory for "Immigration and Naturalization Service." Or call the office in Washington, DC, at 202-514-2000, to find the office nearest you.

The INS will search arrival records for the Western ports, including San Francisco, Seattle, and Honolulu. The records for San Francisco go back to 1892[2]; for Seattle, to 1894; for Honolulu, to 1900 (Hawaii became a United States territory in 1898). Given enough information about an immigrant's arrival, the INS can also search its Alien Registration Records and Naturalization Records. (Remember that *issei* were not allowed to become naturalized citizens until 1952.) These records will show an immigrant's birthdate, his or her age upon arrival, destination in the United States, first occupation, etc.

If an ancestor landed in Hawaii, you might check the Hawaii State Archives. Write them at Ialane Palace Grounds, Honolulu, HI 96813. They have their own records on Japanese immigrants that predate the INS records. Their holdings include ship manifests and passenger manifests. These can tell the name of the ship the subject took, job assignment, emigration company that sponsored him or her, names of relatives, and in some instances the port of departure. These records are also in the holdings of the LDS Library in Salt Lake City.

Another source of immigration information is the office of the Japanese Consulate General in Honolulu, Hawaii, which has records of the arrivals and departures of Japanese immigrants dating back to 1885. Contact the Consulate at 1742 Nuuanu Avenue, Honolulu, HI 96817. You might also try the office of the Japanese Embassy in Washington, DC, 202-939-6700. Also, the library of the University of California at Los Angeles holds more than 100 microfilm reels of Japanese immigration records from the Japanese Foreign Ministry.

The National Archives

The National Archives house millions of records about people who have had dealings with the federal government. In addition to the main facility in Washington, DC, there

---

[2] Some of the pre-1906 records for San Francisco were destroyed in a fire.

are eleven Regional Archives (listed below). Among their holdings, the ones that are most useful to genealogical research are the population censuses, naturalization records, and customs and immigration passenger lists.

Since 1790 the government has taken censuses of the nation's population every ten years. The National Archives have microfilm of the 1880 census, fragments of the 1890 census, and the 1900 and 1910 censuses. These cover the peak period of Japanese immigration. The census will have a card index to entries for each household that included a child aged ten and younger. On the cards are the name, age, and birthplace of each household member. To order a copy from the National Archives you will need to know not only the census in which a person's name appears, but the exact page number. You can look this up in the indexes to the census schedules, which are also in the National Archives. (See *Guide to Genealogical Research in the National Archives.*)

The National Archives also hold partial customs passenger lists and the immigration passenger lists dating back to 1820. These lists tell you the name of the ship an immigrant came aboard and give each person's vital information. Name indexes are available in book form (see **Resources** list). You can use the index to look up an immigrant's name, port of entry, and month and year of arrival. With this information you can file a request with the National Archives for a copy of the list on which the immigrant's name appeared (Form NATF 81, "Order of Copies of Passenger Arrival Records").

The National Archives publish pamphlets and guides to genealogical research and hold workshops for genealogists. For information and all other queries, call or write the Reference Services Branch (NNRS), National Archives, Washington, DC 20408, 202-501-5400. To order publications or microfilm, call, write, or fax the Publications Services Staff (NEPS), Marketing and Fulfillment Branch, National Archives, Washington, DC 20408, 202-501-5240, fax: 202-501-5293. Or you can call or write the Director, National Archives, at the Regional Branch that serves your home state. They are listed below.

Central Plains Region
2312 East Bannister Road
Kansas City, MO 64131
816-926-6272

Research room hours: Monday–Friday, 8 a.m. to 4 p.m., third Thursday of each month, 8 a.m. to 8 p.m. Also open on the third Saturday of each month, 8 a.m. to 4 p.m. Serves Iowa, Kansas, Missouri, and Nebraska.

Great Lakes Region
7358 South Pulaski Road
Chicago, IL 60629
312-581-7816

Research room hours: Monday-Friday, 8 a.m. to 4:15 p.m. Serves Illinois, Indiana, Michigan, Minnesota, Ohio, and Wisconsin.

Mid-Atlantic Region
Ninth and Market Streets, Room 1350
Philadelphia, PA 19107
215-597-3000

Research room hours: Monday–Friday, 8 a.m. to 5 p.m. Also open on the first and third Saturdays of each month, 8 a.m. to 12:00 p.m. Serves Delaware, Pennsylvania, Maryland, Virginia, and West Virginia.

New England Region
380 Trapelo Road
Waltham, MA 02154
617-647-8100

Research room hours: Monday–Friday, 8 a.m. to 4:30 p.m. Also open on the first Saturday of each month, 8 a.m. to 4:30 p.m. Serves Connecticut, Maine, Massachusetts, New Hamphire, Rhode Island, and Vermont.

Northeast Region
Building 22-MOTBY
Bayonne, NJ 07002-5388
201-823-7241

Research room hours: Monday–Friday, 8 a.m. to 4:30 p.m. Also open on the third Saturday of each month, 8 a.m. to 4:00 p.m. Serves New Jersey, New York, Puerto Rico, and the Virgin Islands.

Pacific Northwest Region
6125 Sand Point Way NE
Seattle, WA 98115
206-526-6507

Research room hours: Monday–Friday, 7:45 a.m. to 4 p.m.; one Tuesday each month, 7:45 a.m. to 9 p.m.; one Saturday each month, 12 p.m. to 4 p.m. Serves Alaska, Idaho, Oregon, and Washington.

Pacific Sierra Region
1000 Commodore Drive
San Bruno, CA 94066
415-876-9009

Research room hours: Monday, Tuesday, Thursday, Friday, 7:45 a.m. to 4:15 p.m.; Wednesday, 8 a.m. to 8:30 p.m. Serves Hawaii, Nevada except for Clark County, northern California, and the Pacific Ocean.

Pacific Southwest Region
24000 Avila Road
Laguna Niguel, CA

Mailing address:
P.O. Box 6719
Laguna Niguel, CA 92677-6719
714-643-4241

Research room hours: Monday-Friday, 8 a.m. to 4:30 p.m. Also open on the first Saturday of each month, 8 a.m. to 4:30 p.m. Serves Arizona, southern California, and Clark County, Nevada.

Rocky Mountain Region
Building 48, Denver Federal Center
Denver, CO 80225

or
P.O. Box 25307
Denver, CO 80225
303-236-0818

Research room hours: Monday, Tuesday, Thursday, Friday, 7:30 a.m. to 4 p.m.; Wednesday, 7:30 a.m. to 5 p.m. Serves Colorado, Montana, North Dakota, South Dakota, Utah, and Wyoming.

Southeast Region
1557 St. Joseph Avenue
East Point, GA 30344
404-763-7474 or 763-7477

Research room hours: Monday, Wednesday, Thursday, Friday, 7:30 a.m. to 4:30 p.m.; Tuesday, 9 a.m. to 5 p.m. Also open on the second Saturday of each month, 9 a.m. to 5 p.m. Serves Alabama, Florida, Georgia, Kentucky, Mississippi, North Carolina, South Carolina, Tennessee.

Southwest Region
501 West Felix Street
Fort Worth, TX

Mailing address:
P.O. Box 6216
Fort Worth, TX 76115
817-334-5525

Research room hours: Monday–Friday, 8 a.m. to 4 p.m. Serves Arkansas, Louisiana, New Mexico, Oklahoma, and Texas.

Sources in Japan

As noted above, the Japanese consulate offices can help with records of immigrant arrivals and departures in the United States. But to research genealogies in Japan, one will have to know an immigrant's name and its Chinese characters, or *kanji*, as well as the name of his or her hometown or place of birth.

Research in Japan can be immensely rewarding. Since 1872 Japanese families or households have kept a register of each of their members, called a *koseki*. This is essentially a pedigree chart like the one noted in the previous chapter. It lists each person's name in a family or household and any change of that person's status (adoption, marriage, death, etc.). With a *koseki*, one can trace a person from cradle to grave.

Under the feudal system before the Meiji Restoration of 1868, families in the peasant class did not have surnames. In the Meiji era, however, all families were required to have surnames. Many people simply adopted the names of their homelands, such as Yamaguchi, or geographic names, such as Ogawa (which means "big river").

Koseki are filed by the name of the *koshu* (head of the house) or *hitosha* (first one listed) and the *honseki* (registered hometown or permanent address). Records of people who have died, married, or renounced their Japanese citizenship are withdrawn from a *koseki*; their records are known as *joseki* (withdrawn registers).

To find *koseki* or *joseki*, you will need the name of the family or household head and the locality where they are registered. This can be difficult because many districts, towns, and villages in Japan have changed names over the last century. A number of Japanese reference books list the former and present names of cities, towns, and villages, and the addresses of the government offices of each locality.

Most government offices will try to help, though they will charge a fee. Write clearly in English, and provide all available information about the subject. Give his or her full name, hometown, and birth date (guess, if necessary). Provide a self-addressed envelope with sufficient postage.

Another source is the Buddhist death register, or *kakochō*. In Japan it is common to give the deceased a Buddhist posthumous (in death) name, or vow. This name, which fills up an entire page, is like a poem or eulogy of sorts. It gives vital

Royal or aristocratic families often maintained detailed genealogies. However, some hired genealogists were known to invent ties to nobility that did not really exist in order to please their clients.

information about a person's life. *Kakochō* are kept in Buddhist temples. To find a person's *kakochō*, it is necessary to find the family's temple. Descendants in the United States and Japan, telephone directories, or directories of temples can help.

Other death records include *ihai* (mortuary tablets), which are wooden, oblong tablets with inscriptions similar to those of *kakochō*. These stand on the *butsudan* (family altar). Again, check with descendants here and in Japan whether the family's *ihai* have been kept. A last source is tombstone inscriptions, which give Buddhist death names, their common names, and death dates. You can check an ancestor's tombstone if you are traveling to Japan, or if the person was buried in a Buddhist cemetery in the United States.

You may find it hard to trace a family's roots much beyond the Meiji era. The naming of the peasantry was very confusing and disorganized. As a result, there are more than

100,000 last names in Japan. Some are very common; some are quite rare. For instance, ten years ago there were roughly 2 million people named Sato living in Japan.

Aristocratic or *samurai* families often kept *keizu* or *kafu*, or professionally prepared genealogies. These can go back many centuries. The people who made them, however, were hired by families who wanted to prove their noble status. It was in the preparers' interest to find noble blood ties whether they existed or not. So the farther back a genealogy goes, the more critically you should look at it.

Resources

GENEALOGICAL SOURCES

Ancestry's Guide to Research. Salt Lake City: Ancestry Inc., 1985.

> See *The Source*, p. 117. A beginner's guide to using primary and original sources in a genealogical search.

The Archives: A Guide to the National Archives Field Branches. Salt Lake City: Ancestry Inc., 1988.

> A listing of the holdings of the eleven regional branches of the National Archives.

Arthur, Stephen, and Arthur, Julia. *Your Life & Times: How to Put a Life Story on Tape*. Baltimore: Genealogical Publishing Co., 1987.

> A step-by-step guide to recording your life history on tape. Produce a lively document to share with relatives at holidays and family reunions. You can update your life history at your own convenience.

Bannister, Shala Mills. *Family Treasures: Videotaping Your Family History. A Guide for Preserving Your Family's Living History as an Heirloom for Future Generations*. Baltimore: Clearfield Co., 1994.

> A guide to videotaping your family history. Includes advice on how to videotape as well as on how to interview your family.

Civilian Personnel Records
111 Winnebago Street
St. Louis, MO 63118

Write to this office for information on civilian employees of the U.S. Government after 1909.

Clifford, Karen. *Genealogy and Computers for the Complete Beginner.* **Baltimore: Genealogical Publishing Co., 1992.**

A textbook designed to introduce beginners to computer applications for genealogical research. Includes a guide to software, databases, and local sources.

Croom, Emily Anne. *The Genealogist's Companion and Sourcebook.* **Cincinnati, OH: Betterway Books, 1994.**

A reference guide to sources for a family historian.

Directory of Professional Genealogists. **Salt Lake City: Association of Professional Genealogists, 1994.**

This directory will lead you to professionals in the field of genealogy who, for a fee, will research your family history. If other family members become interested in and supportive of your search, they might be willing to employ the services of a professional to continue the work you have started.

Eakle, Arlene. *Eight Thousand Little-Used Biography and Genealogy Sources.* **Salt Lake City: Genealogical Institute, 1987.**

A guide to obscure and hard to find genealogical sources, for an especially involved family history search.

————. *Tracing the Immigrant Ancestor.* **Salt Lake City: Genealogical Institute, 1973.**

A guide to tracing a family history as far back as the first-generation immigrant ancestor.

Evelyn Spears Family Group Sheet Exchange.

For a ten-dollar fee, this service provides previously researched family group sheets for a requested surname. It has a catalogue of roughly 14,000 surnames. For information write to:

12502 East Fridger Street
Elk, WA 99009

Filby, P. William, ed. *Passenger & Immigration Lists Index: A Reference Guide to Published Lists of about 500,000 Passengers Who Arrived in America in the 17th, 18th, and 19th Centuries,* 3 vols. Detroit: Gale Research Co., 1981.

A comprehensive guide to looking up passenger lists of immigrant ships.

Filby, P. William, and Meyer, Mary K. *Supplement to Passenger & Immigrations List.* Detroit: Gale Research Co., 1987.

An updating of the work listed above.

Genealogist's Address Book. Baltimore: Genealogical Publishing Co., 1991.

A directory of names, addresses, and telephone numbers of organizations and institutions that might help in your search. Arranged by subject, cross-referenced, and alphabetized.

Genealogy Bulletin: American Genealogical Lending Library Newsletter
P.O. Box 329
Bountiful, UT 84011-0329
801-298-5446

Bimonthly journal contains articles on research, queries from subscribers, and the latest publications that can be purchased or borrowed from the library.

Genealogy Digest
Genealogy Digest Magazine, Inc.
P.O. Box 15861
Salt Lake City, UT 84115

Quarterly publication contains member queries and articles of genealogical relevance.

Greenwood, Val D. *The Researcher's Guide to American Genealogy.* **Baltimore: Genealogical Publishing Co., 1990.**

A guide for more advanced family historians, with tips on tracking down obscure sources of information.

Gubler, Greg. "Asian-American Records and Research" in *Ethnic Genealogy: A Research Guide.* **Edited by Jessie Carney Smith. Westport, CT: Greenwood Press, 1983.**

An invaluable guide to researching family history using records both in the United States and Japan. It also gives a summary history of Japanese American immigration.

———. "Family History for Japanese Americans" in *World Conference on Records.* **Salt Lake City: Corporation of the President of The Church of Jesus Christ of Latter-day Saints, 1980.**

A brief introduction to the basic sources and research approaches in both the United States and Japan.

Guide to Genealogical Research in the National Archives, **rev. ed. Washington, DC: The National Archives, 1985.**

A guide to the records housed in the National Archives. Explains what kinds of records are available, what information each record contains, and which are available on microfilm. It also explains how to locate records, request copies, and other research questions.

Hiratsu, Kin-itsu. "The Search for My Japanese Roots: Using Buddhist and Local Sources to Reconstruct Family History" in *World Conference on Records.* **Salt Lake City: Corporation of the President of The Church of Jesus Christ of Latter-day Saints, 1980.**

A doctor who successfully traced his genealogy discusses how he used Buddhist death records and local sources in his search.

Jacobson, Judy. *A Genealogist's Refresher Course.* Baltimore: Clearfield Co., 1995.

Relates first-hand experiences in genealogical research, pointing out dos and don'ts and good sources for information to help in your exploration.

Johnson, Lt. Col. Richard S. *How to Locate Anyone Who Is or Has Been in the Military.* San Antonio, TX: MIE Publishing, 1993.

Outlines various methods for locating a relative who served in the military, and provides addresses and phone numbers of relevant offices.

Kemp, Thomas J. *International Vital Records Handbook*, 3d ed. Baltimore: Genealogical Publishing Co., 1994.

A collection of vital records application forms from around the world.

Kirkham, E. Kay. *A Handy Guide to Record-Searching in the Larger Cities of the United States.* Logan, UT: Everton Publishers, 1974.

A guide to vital records of cities, including street maps and indexes, and other information that can help you trace the life history of an ancestor.

Lainhart, Ann S. *State Census Records.* Baltimore: Genealogical Publishing Co., 1992.

Comprehensive list of state census records. Census records can provide valuable information on household composition.

McNeil, Barbara. *Biography and Genealogy Master Index, 1994.* Detroit: Gale Research Co., 1993.

This up-to-date index of biographies and genealogical sources is an invaluable guide to any family historian.

Muran, Lois Kay. *Family Tree Questionnaire.* **Baltimore: Clearfield Co., 1995.**

Contains fill-in-the-blank forms for recording information on members of your family. The author's forms can provide you with ideas for developing your own.

Neagles, James C., and Neagles, Lila L. *Locating Your Immigrant Ancestor: A Guide to Naturalization Records.* **Logan, UT: Everton Publishers, 1986.**

This book features an index of immigration records listed by state and county, dating back to 1837. It also describes the immigration process and the history of immigration patterns in the United States.

Pence, Richard A. *Computer Genealogy: A Guide to Research Through High Technology.* **Salt Lake City: Ancestry Inc., 1991.**

An introduction to using computers for genealogical research.

Portnov, Vincent. *United States Guide to Family Records: Where and How to Write for Family Records.* **Chicago: Lin-Port House, 1977.**

The "where" of the book, the guide to sources of vital records, is outdated and less useful than the "how"—suggestions on whom to write for information and what questions to ask.

Prezecha, Donna, and Lowrey, Joan. *Guide to Genealogy Software.* **Baltimore: Genealogical Publishing Co., 1993.**

Provides advice for choosing genealogy software. Contains examples of reports from various programs. Software can be a quick and convenient way to organize, store, and update your genealogical findings.

Schweitzer, George Keene. *Handbook of Genealogical Sources.* **Knoxville, TN: G. K. Schweitzer, 1991.**

A bibliography of handbooks and manuals on genealogical research in the United States, this book may lead you to information that answers a particular research question.

Shadrick, Irene. *Libraries for Genealogists.* **Bountiful, UT: Family History Publishers, 1989.**

A guide to library sources useful to a family historian throughout the United States.

Smith, Elsdon C. *American Surnames.* **Baltimore: Genealogical Publishing Co., 1994.**

Explains the roots and meanings of numerous American surnames, including those derived from Asian names.

The Source: A Guide to American Genealogy. **Salt Lake City: Ancestry Inc., 1984.**

A comprehensive guide to genealogical records and source material, especially those housed in the LDS Family History Library in Salt Lake City.

Stryker-Rodda, Harriet. *How to Climb Your Family Tree: Genealogy for Beginners.* **Baltimore: Genealogical Publishing Co., 1993.**

A how-to book to starting your genealogy research.

Tepper, Michael. *American Passenger Arrival Records.* **Baltimore: Genealogical Publishing Co., 1988.**

A guide to the records of immigrants arriving at American ports, including birth registers and passenger lists.

They Came in Ships. **Salt Lake City: Ancestry Inc., 1989.**

A research guide to information and records of immigrant arrivals at the beginning of the twentieth century.

Thorndale, William, and Dollarhide, William. *Map*

Guide to the U.S. Federal Censuses, 1790–1920.
Baltimore: Genealogical Publishing Co., 1991.

Four hundred maps showing all U.S. county boundaries from 1790 to 1920, aiding the genealogical researcher when studying U.S. censuses. Contains an index listing all of the current U.S. counties.

Using Records in the National Archives for Genealogical Research. **General Information Leaflet #5. Washington, DC: National Archives, 1990.**

An overview of the resources of the National Archives and a guide to using them in your research.

Wasserman, P., and Kennington, A., eds. *Ethnic Information Sources of the United States.* **Detroit: Gale Research Co., 1983.**

A comprehensive listing of cultural and educational organizations, heritage institutes, and libraries and archives with ethnic collections.

Webb, Herschel. *Research in Japanese Sources: A Guide.* **New York: Columbia University Press, 1965.**

Somewhat outdated, and written primarily for people doing research in Japanese-language sources, this book nonetheless contains useful information on Japanese naming customs, geographic jurisdictions, and dating methods. It also offers tips for more advanced research.

Wright, Norman Edgar. *Adventures in Genealogy: Case Studies in the Unusual.* **Baltimore: Clearfield Co., 1994.**

A leading genealogist, Wright recounts three of his personal experiences in researching genealogy. Learn from his mistakes and successes.

JAPANESE AMERICAN NEWSPAPERS

Asahi Shinbun International Inc. **(Japanese, daily)**
757 Third Avenue
New York, NY 10017

or: 19300 South Hamilton Avenue
Gardena, CA 90248

Chicago Shimpo (Japanese and English, biweekly)
Japanese American News
4670 North Manor Avenue
Chicago, IL 60625

Hawaii Herald (English, bimonthly)
Hawaii Hochi Ltd.
917 Kokea Street
Honolulu, HI 96817-4528

Hawaii Hochi (Japanese and English, daily)
917 Kokea Street
Honolulu, HI 96817-4528

Hawaii Pacific Press (Japanese and English, monthly)
P.O. Box 3596
Honolulu, HI 96811

Hokubei Hochi (Japanese, three times a week)
P.O. Box 3173
Seattle, WA 98114

Hokubei Mainichi (Japanese and English, daily)
1746 Post Street
San Francisco, CA 94115

International Times (Japanese, semimonthly)
4655 Ruffner Street
San Diego, CA 92111

Nichi Bei Times (Japanese and English, daily)
2211 Bush Street
San Francisco, CA 94115

While the following newspapers are no longer published, microfilm copies are available at some libraries.

California
Hokubei Asahi (North American Sun). San Francisco.

University of California, Berkeley, Library.

Kashu Mainichi (California State Daily). Los Angeles.

University of California at Los Angeles (UCLA) Library.

Nichibei (Japanese American News). San Francisco.

California State Library and University of California, Berkeley, Library.

Ofu Nippo (Sacramento Daily News). Sacramento.

California State Library and University of California, Berkeley, Library.

Pacific Citizen. Los Angeles.

Library of Congress.

Rafu Shimpo (Los Angeles Daily Japanese News). Los Angeles.

UCLA Library and University of Southern California Library.

Shin Sekai (New World Daily News). San Francisco.

University of California, Berkeley, Library.

Shin Sekai Asahi (New World-Sun). San Francisco.

University of California, Berkeley, Library and the Library of Congress.

Colorado
Kakushi Jiji (Colorado Times). Denver.

Library of Congress.

Rocky Mountain Jiho (Rocky Mountain Post). Denver.

Library of Congress.

Hawaii
Hawaii Mainichi Shinbun and Hilo Times (for copies, write to K. Okubo, P.O. Box 306, Hilo, HI 96721)

Nippu Jiju (also called *Hawaii Times*). Honolulu.

The LDS Family History Library in Salt Lake City, the University of Hawaii (Honolulu) Library, and the Hawaii State Archives.

New York
**New York Nichibei (*Japanese American News*).
New York.**

New York Public Library.

Utah
Utah Nippo. Salt Lake City.

University of Utah Library and the Library of Congress.

Washington
Asahi News (*The Sun*). Seattle.

Washington State University Library and the University of Illinois (Urbana) Library.

Hokubei Jiji (*North American Times*). Seattle.

Library of Congress.

Japanese American Courier. Seattle.

University of Washington Library.

Taihoku Nippo (*Great North Daily News*). Seattle.

University of Washington Library and the Library of Congress.

JAPAN-AMERICA SOCIETIES

Japan-America societies are American organizations interested in the relationship between Japan and the United States. While each society functions differently, many offer cultural programs that may be of interest to you as you learn about Japanese culture. Some have resource libraries and programs such as language instruction. Contact a Japan-

America society near you to find out what kinds of resources they may offer. The staff may be able to give you advice on Japanese genealogical research, or put you in touch with others doing similar work.

National Association of Japan-America Societies
333 East 47th Street
New York, NY 10017

The Japan America Society of Alabama
Alabama World Business Center
1500 Resource Drive
Birmingham, AL 35242

Japan-American Society of Arkansas
The Arkansas International Center
University of Arkansas at Little Rock
2801 South University
Little Rock, AR 72204

The Japan Society of Boston, Inc.
22 Batterymarch Street
Boston, MA 02109

Japan-America Society of Charlotte
Office of International Programs
UNC Charlotte
Charlotte, NC 29223

Japan America Society of Chicago, Inc.
225 West Wacker Drive, Suite 2250
Chicago, IL 60606

Japan-America Society of Greater Cincinnati
300 Carew Tower
441 Vine Street
Cincinnati, OH 45202-2812

Japan Society of Cleveland
Asia Plaza 210B
2999 Payne Avenue
Cleveland, OH 44115

Japan America Society of Colorado
1200 17th Street, Suite 3000
Denver, CO 80202

Japan America Society of Dallas/Fort Worth
P.O. Box 58095
Dallas, TX 75258

Japan-America Society of Florida, Inc.
Belleview Mido Resort-Palm Cottage
25 Bellview Boulevard
P.O. Box 2317
Clearwater, FL 34617

Japan-America Society of Georgia
Suite 710, South Tower
225 Peachtree Street NE
Atlanta, GA 30303

Greater Detroit and Windsor Japan-America Society
Suite 1500, 150 West Jefferson Street
Detroit, MI 48226

Japan-America Society of Hawaii
P.O. Box 1412
Honolulu, HI 96806

Japan-America Society of Houston
Suite 1760
1360 Post Oak Boulevard
Houston, TX 77056

Japan-America Society of Indiana, Inc.
Merchants Bank Building
11 South Meridien Street
Suite 200
Indianapolis, IN 46206-3509

Japan/America Society of Kentucky
P.O. Box 333
Lexington, KY 40584

Japan America Society of Minnesota
43 Main Street SE
Suite EH-401, Riverplace
Minneapolis, MN 55414

Japan-America Society of Nevada
P.O. Box 26267
Las Vegas, NV 89126-0267

Japan-America Society of New Hampshire
P.O. Box 1226
Portsmouth, NH 03802-1226

Japan Society, Inc.
333 East 47th Street
New York, NY 10017

Japan Society of Northern California
312 Sutter Street, 4F
San Francisco, CA 94108

North Carolina Japan Center
North Carolina State University
Box 8112
Raleigh, NC 27695-8112

Japan-America Society of Oregon
221 NW Second Avenue
Portland, OR 97209

Japan-America Society of Pennsylvania
500 Wood Street
20th Floor
Pittsburgh, PA 15222

Japan-America Society of Greater Philadelphia
1818 Market Street, Suite 3510
Philadephia, PA 19103

Japan America Society of Southern California
ARCO Plaza, Level C
505 South Flower Street
Los Angeles, CA 90071

Japan Society of South Florida
World Trade Center, 2809
80 SW Eighth Street
Miami, FL 33130

Japan America Society of St. Louis, Inc.
7 North Brentwood Boulevard
St. Louis, MO 63105

Japan-America Society of the State of Washington
1800 Ninth Avenue, Suite 1550
Seattle, WA 98101-1322

Japan-Virginia Society
Suite 304
830 East Main Street
Richmond, VA 23219

Japan-America Society of Washington, Inc.
1020 19th Street NW
Lower Level
Washington, DC 20036

Japan-America Society of Wisconsin, Inc.
756 North Milwaukee Street
Milwaukee, WI 53202

Chapter 4
Oral History

What Is Oral History?

An oral history interview is different from the interviews described in Chapter 3. Those interviews are used to fill out a family group chart or pedigree chart. An informant is asked questions of fact: when was a person born, where did he or she live, what is that person's full name, etc. These are called "closed-end" questions.

By contrast, the questions of the oral history are "open-ended." There are no right or wrong "answers," only responses. Open questions are meant only to introduce topics of discussion. The informant is given the chance to reminisce or meditate on certain topics. The oral history tends to be more personal.

An example of a closed-end question to a person might be: Where were you born? An open-end question might be: What was your hometown like when you were growing up? Recalling the journalist's five Ws, one could say that closed-end questions more often begin with *where, when, who.* Open-end questions might begin with any of those, as well as *how*—for instance, *how did you feel when you graduated from high school?* These are, of course, not hard and fast rules.

Just as there are two types of questions, there are two types of oral histories. One is autobiographical. The informant is basically recounting the story of his or her life. The other type is topical. The informant talks about a particular person, an event, a place, or even a common belief. A Japanese American informant might share memories of daily life in an internment camp during World War II or of growing up in the 1960s. A topical oral history tends to be less open-ended than an autobiographical oral history.

Talking to elderly relatives may reveal fascinating information about the lives of *issei* and *nisei*.

Oral history can be fascinating and valuable. It can also be extremely difficult. As the name suggests, it is something that is done only live, or "orally." Therefore, how you treat an interviewee, or *informant*, can determine the success or failure of a project.

Preparations

The first step is to choose your informant. Anyone can give an oral history—family members, friends, neighbors, colleagues, teachers, peers. You should begin with the person closest to you. As you gather more and more information, you can move on to less familiar people, even strangers. And as you gain experience you can begin interviewing people who might be less open, or less eager to reminisce about the past.

Ask for an appointment well in advance. Plan to keep the session short: one or two hours at most. If more time is needed (and all goes well), follow-up sessions should be arranged. Do not be discouraged if someone refuses to be interviewed. Many people are shy about giving oral histories, or feel that they have no interesting stories to tell. Ask again. Explain clearly why his or her stories are interesting and important to you. Agree to keep any or all of an oral history session confidential, and stick to that agreement. But do not badger. Remember, no one *has* to grant you an interview.

Interviews are best conducted in a quiet, private setting. Usually the informant's home is best. The interview should be scheduled for a time in the day when the informant can speak to you without interruption or disturbance. Ideally, no one else should be present for the interview. A third party can hinder the flow of the interview.

If you wish to audiotape the interview, a microcassette recorder is probably best. Because it is so small, the informant is less likely to be intimidated by it; he or she may even forget about it in the course of the interview. Most models have microphones sensitive enough to pick up voices well beyond arms' length. The recorder should be placed on a flat surface such as a tabletop (not on the floor) between you and the informant.

If you are videotaping the interview, you will need a tripod and a remote with which to activate the camcorder. For camera setup, lighting, sound levels, and other technical matters, see Duane and Pat Sturm's *Video Family History* or William P. Fletcher's *Recording Your Family History*, listed in the **Resources.**

It is important to ask the informant beforehand whether he or she agrees to be recorded. Do not surprise anyone by showing up with a camcorder or pulling out a tape recorder at the last minute. A person has the right to refuse to be recorded. If a person does not wish to be recorded, you can take thorough notes of the interview with pencil and notebook. But whether the interview is taped or not, you should always keep written notes during the interview.

Write or call the informant a day or two before the appointment. Thank him or her once more and briefly mention the topics that you would like to cover in the interview. This will give the person time to reflect on things he or she might not have thought of in a long time. Do not read off the questions you plan to ask, however. Otherwise the informant might feel compelled to rehearse answers.

The Interview

Do not arrive for an appointment and jump right into the interview. Take a few minutes to chat as you set up equipment and get organized.

If the interview is being recorded, start the tape with a brief introduction, such as the following:

> This is [informant's name] oral history interview with [your name], at [location of interview session, including full address], on [month, date, year].

Before proceeding, play back the introduction to make sure the equipment is recording properly.

The sequence of questions is important to make the informant comfortable. Do not begin with a sensitive or

In interviews, you might want to ask relatives about what kinds of jobs they have held. In Hawaii, for example, many Japanese American women operated gas stations.

potentially embarrassing question. That could dampen the rest of the interview. Instead start with an easy question about a topic that the informant will not mind discussing at length. If the person has a hobby or a special interest, you might ask how it started, for example.

The first question can go a long way toward making the informant comfortable and open. It shows your genuine interest in his or her story. The informant's answer can lead to other topics that can be discussed later. The first question can also help the informant figure out what to emphasize and what to leave out, how to arrange his or her memories into a narrative.

The first question should be easy, but not insulting. A silly question such as "What's your favorite color?" can put off an informant as easily as a tough one. Never belittle your informant.

Questions should be brief and simple. They should not have multiple parts: for instance, "Did you attend college and if so, which schools did you apply to and which one did you attend?" The interview is an oral history, not an oral examination. Nor should a question contain any assumptions or preconceptions. This is called begging the question. For instance, "What was it like growing up in a boring small town in the Midwest?" assumes that the person's hometown was boring; he or she might think otherwise.

As interviewer, you should refrain from voicing opinions. Avoid loaded words and questions that seem to make value judgments. Consider the example below:

How did you feel about having to settle for being a housewife? The phrase *having to settle* implies that being a housewife is a kind of failure. Whether or not you believe that, keep it to yourself. A better way to phrase the same question might be:

How did it feel to get married?

And never get into an argument with an informant. If he or she has stated something contrary to what you know, ask again. Do not confront the person or get into a debate. You gain nothing by showing someone up with how much you know.

Questioning

Though it is important to have a list of questions ready, you should not be bound by any script. Be prepared for the unexpected. An informant's response might spin off new questions. He or she might reveal a crucial insight or piece of new information. One might wish to know more detail about a particular point. An informant might state a belief or idea that needs explanation.

Do not, however, interrupt a person with questions or comments. Instead, write them down in your notebook and follow up later in the interview. Notes should be brief—in shorthand, if you know how; otherwise, a few words at most. If someone is telling an interesting anecdote about walking to school every morning and you want to know how far the walk was, you might write: "home to school: far?" (how far was it from home to school). If the informant pauses, do not jump in immediately with a new question. Do not be afraid of moments of silence. Give the person some time to think.

Taking notes during an interview serves four purposes. One, it prevents you from repeating questions. Two, it helps to structure the rest of the interview. Three, it highlights what the informant emphasizes and what he or she leaves out, which tells what he or she considers important. Finally, it shows the informant that you are listening with interest.

Do not, however, bury your nose in a notebook. Maintain eye contact with the informant as much as possible. This is not only good manners. An informant's response to a question or topic is not only in his or her words, but in his or her gestures as well. Observe closely the facial expression, the body posture, eye movements. Listen also to the tone and volume of voice. These can indicate what a person is thinking or feeling.

As mentioned above, sensitive questions should be saved for later. Questions concerning death, money, divorce, health, and other highly private matters should be handled with utmost care. Wait until the interview is well under way to raise them. Do not wait too long, however. If you wait for the end of the interview to ask difficult questions, the informant may be tired and impatient by then, and give you tired and impatient answers.

Possible Topics

Ask questions specific to the topic that the informant can answer. For instance, you might ask a Japanese American informant who grew up in an internment camp about conditions, schooling, recreational activities, his or her feelings about the camp guards. Someone who grew up on a sugar plantation in Hawaii can tell you how workers lived. A former picture bride can tell you how it felt to come to the United States to marry a stranger. A *nisei* informant can talk about growing up with *issei* parents.

For an autobiographical interview, however, the possibilities are much more open, less specific. Listed below are some ideas.

A. Childhood and Youth

- Recollections of self: likes and dislikes, abilities and disabilities, sicknesses, role(s) at home, memorable anecdotes
- Recollections of family members: personalities, physical descriptions, idiosyncrasies, memorable anecdotes
- Living situation during childhood: description of residence, household, financial situation, memorable anecdotes
- Customs: Japanese customs, food, dress, as part of everyday life; memorable anecdotes
- Language: was Japanese spoken in home? Japanese school or lessons?
- Education: teachers, friends, school buildings, classrooms, transportation, classes, activities, hobbies, honors, memorable anecdotes
- Childhood games, activities outside school
- Social life in childhood, teens
- Travel: memorable trips, vacations, or other travel;

include destinations, fellow travelers, persons encoun-
tered, and memorable anecdotes
- Hobbies, interests, habits
- Religious practices
- Holidays: Japanese and American holidays observed
- Hometown: where, scenery, population, economic
  activity, landmarks, local lore
- Civic events, activities, organizations: parades, picnics,
  carnivals, etc.

B. Adulthood

(Find out beforehand whether any of these topics apply to
the informant)

- Marriage and family: courtship, wedding, marriage,
  having children
- College or technical school: goals, school(s) attended,
  interests, curricula, degrees and honors, instructors,
  obstacles encountered, memorable anecdotes
- Military service: which branch, drafted or enlisted,
  basic training, postings, combat duty, friends, com-
  rades, officers, memorable anecdotes
- Vocations and careers: jobs held, ambitions, goals, job
  changes, job description, memorable anecdotes
- Travel: trips to Japan; purpose of Japan visits; other
  destinations
- Retirement

C. External Forces

- Remembrances of historic events: e.g., the Great
  Depression, World War II, the assassination of John
  F. Kennedy, the Sixties, Watergate, the Iran hostage
  crisis, the Challenger explosion, etc.
- Changes seen during lifetime: e.g., fashions, technology, community standards, laws, politics, the
  economy, the population

D. Other Topics

- Japanese legends, folktales, myths, commonly held beliefs of family, community
- Superstitions: Japanese lore, local lore
- Traditional Japanese ceremonies, holidays celebrated
- Greatest joys and greatest sorrows
- Advice for younger generations

Ending the Interview

When the informant has nothing more to say, it is time to conclude the interview. Stop the tape recorder or camcorder and rewind the tape. While it is rewinding, review factual items such as dates and the spelling of names with the informant. Make sure the tape box is properly labeled: informant's name, interviewer's name, date, time, location, tape speed (for VHS tapes and microcassette tapes).

Also have the informant sign an interview release stating that: 1) the informant is aware that the interview has been taped and consents; 2) the informant gives permission to the interviewer to use either the tape or the transcript of the interview as the interviewer wishes. Ask the informant before the interview whether he or she will sign such a release, but do not have him or her actually sign it until after the interview is complete. This gives the person a chance to change his or her mind after giving the interview.

A release form can look something like this:

> I, _____,
> consent to have my interview with [your name] recorded on audio / video (circle one) tape, and voluntarily grant permission to [your name] for full use of the interview for whatever purpose he or she may have, in consideration of which I may have a typed copy of the interview upon request.
>
> _____ date: _____
> [informant's signature]

As stated in the introduction, you do not have the right to embarrass or cause pain to anyone with any information you uncover. An interview release does not change that.

Transcribing and Editing an Interview

Printed transcripts of the interview are extremely useful. They can be easily copied and distributed. Handwritten transcripts can also be copied, but transcribing by hand is an enormous task; also, some people may have trouble reading your handwriting. Transcribing an interview on a computer or a typewriter is best. If you cannot type, professional typists can transcribe from tapes for a fee, usually around two to five dollars per page.[1]

If you transcribe the interview, follow certain guidelines. The transcript should be double-spaced, with one-inch margins on the top, bottom, and sides of the page. The informant and interviewer are both identified by their initials.

First, listen to the interview and type as verbatim (word for word) as possible. However, hemming and hawing, repetitions, false starts, can be edited out. Consider the example below.

> AB (informant): Hmm, let's see, well, um, heh heh, what was the home like, let's see. . . . Ah, lemme tell ya, we didn't have a lot of creature comforts, you know what I'm saying? Not a lot of creature comforts. Not a lot, no sir.

AB's response to the question can be edited thus:

> Let me tell you, we didn't have a lot of creature comforts, you know what I'm saying?

In editing a transcript it is important not to change the meaning of an informant's responses. You can edit out extraneous words and exclamations, but only to a point. If

---

[1] Many typists work out of their homes and are not listed in the *Yellow Pages*. They often advertise their services with flyers on bulletin boards in bookstores, libraries, and especially on college campuses.

you collect more than one oral history, they should not all sound the same. People have unique ways of expressing themselves. They utter phrases or even sounds that may not have much literal meaning, but convey a personality, a spirit, that should not be lost in editing.

Exclamations and gestures can also be full of meaning. Laughter, a snort of anger, a deep sigh of sadness—these are not words, but they convey strong feelings and should be recorded on a transcript, in either brackets or parentheses. For example:

> CD [you]: How did you feel when you heard the news of the bombing of Pearl Harbor?
> AB: [Sigh]. Like somebody punched me in the stomach.

Or:

> CD: Do you have any funny stories about your grandfather?
> AB: [Scratches head]. Let's see. Oh, I know one. [Smile]. Oh, you'll like this. [Laughter]. Yes, this is a very funny story. [More laughter, slaps knee]. . . .

As you edit the transcript, play the tape back and listen again. If a word is unclear, leave a blank or type "[word unclear]." Double check the spelling of proper names. Then print out or retype the transcript. The first page of the transcript should be a title page: [INFORMANT'S NAME], Oral History Interview with [YOUR NAME], date, location.

Send a copy to the informant. Ask the person to feel free to correct mistakes or clarify anything that might be confusing. Keep a hard copy in your notebook or in the file for the informant's family group.

The cassettes or VHS tapes should be labeled and stored properly. Read the manufacturer's instructions about proper storage on the packaging.

Resources

HOW TO DO AN ORAL HISTORY

Banaka, William H. *Training in Depth Interviewing.*
New York: Harper & Row, 1971.

A guide to effective interviewing, with tips on preparation, organization, and questioning.

Fletcher, William P. *Recording Your Family History.*
New York: Dodd, Mead and Co., 1983.

A guide to conducting an autobiographical, or "life history," interview for audio or video tape. Includes advice on interviewing techniques and list of suggested topics.

Harvey, Joanne H. *The Living Record: Interviewing and Other Techniques for Genealogists.* **Lansing, MI: J. H. Harvey, 1985.**

An instructive book on using oral history in a genealogical search, with tips on interviewing.

Lichtman, Allan J. "How to Do Oral History" in *Your Family History.* **New York: Vintage, 1978.**

A guide to conducting, recording, and interpreting oral history interviews.

Moss, William W. *Oral History Program Manual.*
New York: Praeger, 1974.

A guide to setting up an oral history project, with helpful suggestions for interviewers.

Payne, Stanley L. *The Art of Asking Questions.* **Princeton, NJ: Princeton University Press, 1951.**

Just what the title promises: a guide to asking questions in an interview, with useful suggestions on wording questions.

Shumway, Gary L., and Hartley, William G. *An Oral History Primer.* **Salt Lake City: Primer Publications, 1973.**

A simple and practical guide to conducting oral history interviews, from the preliminary stages to transcribing interview records. Includes sample topics for an interview. (Note: the section on recording equipment is outdated.)

Stano, Michael E., and Reinsch, N. L. Jr. *Communication in Interviews.* **Englewood Cliffs, NJ: Prentice-Hall, 1982.**

An instructive guide to interview techniques.

Sturm, Duane, and Sturm, Pat. *Video Family History.* **Salt Lake City: Ancestry Inc., 1989.**

A beginner's guide to directing and producing a family documentary with a single video camera. With tips on equipment and film techniques such as editing and dubbing.

Vansina, Jan. *Oral Tradition: A Study in Historical Methodology.* **London: Routledge, 1965.**

Considered a classic study of the art of preserving oral histories.

JAPANESE AMERICAN ORAL HISTORY

Chang, Thelma. *"I Can Never Forget": Men of the 100th/442nd.* **Honolulu: Sigi Productions, 1991.**

The experiences of the *nisei* who served in the 100th Battalion and 442nd Combat Team in World War II, as told by themselves.

Gesenway, Deborah, and Roseman, Mindy. *Beyond Words: Images from America's Concentration Camps.* **Ithaca, NY: Cornell University Press, 1987.**

A collection of paintings, drawings, oral histories, and narratives that capture life in the internment camps during World War II.

Matsuo, Dorothy. *Boyhood to War: History and Anecdotes of the 442nd Regimental Combat Team.* **Honolulu: Mutual Publishing, 1992.**

The story of the 442nd Combat Team, as remembered by its veterans, as well as personal anecdotes of growing up *nisei* in the years preceding World War II.

Tateishi, John. *And Justice for All: An Oral History of the Japanese American Detention Camps.* **New York: Random House, 1984.**

A collection of personal anecdotes and remembrances by *issei* and *nisei* who lived through the ordeal of relocation and internment in World War II.

JAPANESE ORAL HISTORY

Cook, Haruko Taya, and Cook, Theodore F. *Japan at War: An Oral History.* **New York: New Press, 1992.**

A collection of oral histories of ordinary people in Japan recalling their experiences during World War II.

Chapter 5
Some Questions

Terms of Kinship

Terms of kinship define a person's relationship to another person. Some are obvious: *father, mother, grandfather, grandmother, brother, sister, aunt, uncle.* Some are less familiar. *Sibling* is a general term for a brother or sister. *Birth* or *natal parents* are the parents who conceived a person. *Paternal* refers to the father's side of a family: for example, a *paternal grandfather* is a father's father. *Maternal* refers to the mother's side: a *maternal grandmother* is a mother's mother.

Cousins are perhaps the most complicated. Their relationship to a person is qualified by a number. A rule of thumb would be to take the cousin's parents and add one, one being the same generation as the subject's (or your) parents. For instance, a *first cousin* is the child of a parent's sibling (aunt or uncle); a *second cousin* is the child of a parent's *first* cousin; a *third cousin* is the child of a parent's *second* cousin; and so on. Cousins of different generations are said to be at a *remove.* For instance, a first cousin *once removed* is the child of a first cousin. A first cousin *twice removed* is the grandchild of a first cousin. A second cousin *once removed* is the child of a second cousin; a second cousin *twice removed* is the grandchild of a second cousin; and so on.

The parents of one's first cousin, of course, are *aunt* and *uncle.* But one's *great-aunt* or *great-uncle* is the sister or brother of one's grandparents. First cousins share one set of grandparents, either paternal or maternal. A *great-grandparent* is the parent of a grandparent, and a *great-great* aunt or uncle is the sibling of a *great-grandparent. Great* signifies one more generation back.

The Japanese term for grandmother is *obā*.

Half brothers or *half sisters* are siblings who share one *natal* parent—for example, two people born to the same father but different mothers. *Stepsiblings* are siblings who have no natal parent in common. For example, a man and a woman marry for the second time and each has a daughter from the previous marriage. The two daughters are *stepsisters* to one another. The father is the mother's daughter's *stepfather* and the mother is the father's daughter's *stepmother*.

In Japanese, terms of kinship can get complicated. The Japanese spoken language is ordered around a system known as *keigo*, "levels of politeness." This means that the words one uses can change depending on whom one is addressing or talking about.

For instance, the word for one's own parents is *ryōshin*. But when you refer to somebody else's parents, you call them *go-ryōshin*. The word for one's own father is *chichi*. The polite form of father is *otō-san*. You would never call your father "*chichi*" to his face; you would call him *otō-san*. But if you are talking *about* him to someone else, you call him *chichi*. If you are talking about somebody else's father, you call him *otō-san*.

Similarly, the word for your mother is *haha*. The polite form is *okā-san*. You would address your mother or refer to somebody else's mother as *okā-san*. But when talking about your mother to somebody else, you call her *haha*.

The terms for grandparents appear simpler, but they too can be confusing. A grandmother is *obā*, and a grandfather is *ojii*. When addressing your grandparents directly, or talking about somebody else's grandparents, you call them *obā-san* and *ojii-san*. Simple, right? But look at the word for aunt, *oba*, and the word for uncle, *oji*. The only differences are the extra syllables in *oba* and *ojii*. Be careful with pronunciation, so as not to confuse grandparents with aunts and uncles.

An aunt is *oba*; when addressing her or referring to somebody else's aunt, use *oba-san*. Similarly, an uncle is *oji*, but use *oji-san* when addressing him directly or talking about somebody else's uncle.

There are different words for older siblings and younger siblings. An older brother is *ani* or the polite form, *onii-san*; a younger brother is *otōto*, or the polite form, *otōto-san*. An older sister is *ane*, or the polite form, *onee-san*; a younger sister is *imōto* or the polite form, *imōto-san*. (Note: older siblings do not address younger siblings as *otōto-san* or *imōto-san*; they just call them by the first name).

The word for son is *musuko*. The word for an eldest son is *chonan*. The word for daughter is *musume*. An eldest daughter is *chōjō*. The terms for eldest children are important, since traditionally they succeed their parents as heads of households. Typically after the death of a father, the eldest son inherits the family home, while his younger brothers move out to start their own households.

Nontraditional Families

The concept of the American family has changed. We know that the traditional image of family—mother, father, children—is only one of many shapes that families take. The reality is that married couples divorce; parents raise children on their own, without spouses; children are adopted or live away from their parents. Family groups are not always limited to blood kin. Some are formed in response to their particular situations and needs.

In the early 1970s sociologist Carol B. Stack studied a community called the Flats. The Flats were composed of households that banded together in order to survive. The daily chores of living were shared among all the households. Each household was flexible; people moved from home to home. Families were made up not only of blood relatives, but also friends and neighbors who assumed traditional family roles, such as aunt and uncle. Children were raised by the community. Parental duties were shared by several people, not just the mother and father.[1]

When you conduct your genealogical research, keep in mind that the families may include members not related by

---

[1] Carol B. Stack, *All Our Kin* (New York: Harper & Row, 1974).

blood. The pedigree chart described earlier is useful only for tracing a person's direct ancestors. It does not account for others who might have had significant roles in that person's life. While strictly speaking, professional genealogists include only blood relatives on a family tree, it is also true that nonblood relatives can be part of one's family history and oral tradition. Thus it is often helpful to trace them as well. The surest way to account for nonrelated family members is by interviewing people close to and in the family. They can tell you what documents and records cannot. After all, what good is it to track down, say, Ms. N's great-great-aunt from the nineteenth century and know nothing about the family friend who raised Ms. N until she was a teenager?

Adoption

As was stated in the introduction, exploring your family's past is really exploring your own past. The more you know about your ancestors, the more you know about yourself. So if you are adopted, you might want to study both your adopted family and the family or families of your birth parent or parents. Or, you might have a friend or relative who was adopted and wants to know more about his or her past.

Tracing the birth parents of adoptees can be complicated, however. When a person is adopted, he or she is given a new birth certificate. In all but one state, Alabama, records of adoptions are sealed, which means that by law no one, not even the adoptee, can look at them.

Be sensitive to your adoptive parents' feelings when approaching them for information. Assure them that you are only interested in tracing your roots, not in finding a new family. The first step is to ask an adoptive parent or parents: what were the birth parents' names? Where was the adoptee born? Did the birth parents have family there? How old was the adoptee at the time of adoption? What did the birth parent or parents do for a living? Use the family group sheet or questionnaire for questions to ask.

Remember, it is up to adoptive parents to decide how much of what they know about the birth parents to reveal.

They may in fact know very little. But if they are not yet prepared to share certain details about the adoption, do not force the issue. Instead, take what leads or clues they do provide and go from there. Ask family members, friends, neighbors who might be familiar with the circumstances of the adoption. As with any search, record what information you gather on a family group sheet, and keep notes on further leads in your notebook.

Who and *where* are the two most important questions in finding birth parents. With this information you can look up old telephone directories from the adoptee's place of birth, or birth parents' last known hometown. These are usually kept in local public libraries, so you would have to travel to that town or city, or contact the library of that town by telephone or mail.

Local newspapers can also be helpful. If you can find out *when* the adoptee was born, as well as *where*, you can check back issues of the local newspapers for a birth announcement. You can also look up the name of a birth parent or parents in the newspaper's index.

People move around. You may discover the birth parents' hometown only to find they moved on years ago. If you are able to find out the birth parents' old address from a telephone book or other source, you can then go to the United States Post Office. Ask for and fill out a Freedom of Information Request / Address Search Request. You can make this request only if you know their full former address.

There are a number of national organizations that help adoptees search for their birth parents. Perhaps the largest is the Adoptees' Liberty Movement Association (ALMA), listed in **Resources**. This organization was founded by Florence Fisher, an adoptee who successfully found her birth parents after a twenty-year search. ALMA also collects and disseminates information about effective research techniques and conducts workshops to help researchers. Another source, *People Searching News,* is a newsletter for people who are searching for lost or missing family members. It has a hotline that offers free assistance and referrals.

The laws that keep adoption records closed are not intended to punish or hurt anyone; in fact, they are meant to protect. People have all kinds of reasons for putting children up for adoption. In some cases, it is best for everyone involved to keep the identity of a birth parent or parents secret. Though such rules may not be at all appropriate to your situation—and may seem terribly unfair to you—laws cannot allow exceptions. They must be applied to all in order to protect the few.

For an adoptee, it is only natural curiosity to wonder about one's birth parents. Remember the Japanese saying quoted in chapter two: *Umi no oya yori mo sodate no oya* (Your adopted parents are your true parents). Their experiences have shaped them, made them into who they are—the very people who chose to bring their adopted child into their home and lives, to care for and nurture him or her.

Resources

FAMILY ISSUES

Askin, Jayne, with Molly Davis. *Search: A Handbook for Adoptees and Birthparents*, 2d ed. Phoenix, AZ: Oryx Press, 1992.

> Provides listings, sources, and advice on adoptee searches, including family issues, laws, and potential difficulties.

Lifton, Betty Jean. *Lost and Found.* New York: HarperCollins, 1988.

> A personal account of the logistical and emotional hurdles in an adoptee's search for her birth parents.

Marcus, Clare. *Adopted? A Canadian Guide for Adopted Adults in Search of Their Origins.* Vancouver, Canada: International Self-Counsel Press, 1979.

> A guide to sources and tips on searching for adoptees raised in the United States but born in Canada.

Miller, Naomi. *Single Parents by Choice: A Growing Trend in Family Life.* New York: Insight Books, 1992.

> A book that explains why parents choose single-parent situations for themselves and their children. This may shed light on your own family history.

People Searching News.

> A bimonthly newsletter for adoptees, birth parents, and brothers and sisters trying to find biological relatives. If you were adopted, this may be a useful resource.

J. E. Carlson and Associates
P.O. Box 22611
Fort Lauderdale, FL 33335
305-370-7100

Sadler, Judith DeBoard. *Families in Transition: An Annotated Bibliography.* **Hamden, CT: Archon Books, 1988.**

A reference guide to information on nontraditional families, including books published by support groups.

**Social Security Administration
Office of Central Records Operations
Baltimore, MD 21201**

To find a living relative, use Form SSA-L997 to request his or her Social Security application. (Note: Your request may be denied by the Administration.)

Social Security Administration. *Death Master File.*

To find late relatives, check file of deaths on microform in the LDS Family History Centers. Check with your nearest branch, or the main branch.

LDS Family History Library
35 North West Temple Street
Salt Lake City, UT 84150

Wagonseller, William R., et al. *Coping in a Single-Parent Home,* **rev. ed. New York: Rosen Publishing Group, 1995.**

This book includes a helpful discussion for children in single-parent families who are considering seeking the missing parent.

Witherspoon, Mary Ruth. "How to Conduct an Adoption Search" in *Everton's Genealogical Helper,* **July/August, 1994.**

An article by a woman whose successful search for her biological family led to her discovery of 300 living relatives.

SUPPORT GROUPS, REGISTERS, ADVOCATES

Adopted and Searching / Adopted-Birthparent
Reunion Registry
401 East 74th Street
New York, NY 10021
212-988-0110

Adoptees and Birthparents in Search
P.O. Box 5551
West Columbia, SC 29171
803-796-4508

Adoptees' Liberty Movement Association (ALMA)
P.O. Box 154 Washington Bridge Station
New York, NY 10033
212-581-1568

Adoptees' Search Right Association
Xenia, OH 45383
419-855-8439

Adoptees Together
Route 1, Box 30-B5
Climax, NC 27233

Adoptive Families of America
3333 Highway 100 North
Minneapolis, MN 55422
24-hour hotline: 800-372-3300

American Adoption Congress
1000 Connecticut Avenue NW
Washington, DC 20036

Concerned United Birth Parents
200 Walker Street
Des Moines, IA 50317

International Soundex Reunion Registry
P.O. Box 2312
Carson City, NV 89702

FILM

Portrait of My Mother (Haha no shozo).

A documentary about Tsuyoshi Matsumoto, who was born to an American soldier and a Japanese woman in Nagasaki shortly after the end of World War II. Placed in an orphanage at the age of two, he was adopted by an American couple and brought to the United States. Forty years later he returned to Nagasaki to find his biological mother. (Japanese, with English subtitles).

Chapter 6
Wrapping Up Your Research

Family Tree

At all stages of the research you should keep an updated family tree. A family tree is similar to the pedigree charts mentioned earlier. But while the pedigree charts start with someone contemporary (such as yourself) and work backward, the family tree starts at the beginning—that is, the earliest ancestor you have located—and moves forward to the present. Also, the pedigree chart shown in chapter 3 proceeds horizontally (left to right). Typically family trees are organized vertically.

But family trees, like families, take different shapes; no two are alike. Generally family trees contain fewer details about each person than a pedigree chart. They are intended as outlines to illustrate lines of descent and/or relationships. Try to keep people of the same generation on the same line, or tier, in the tree. Do not try to fit an entire family on one family tree; instead, draw up separate ones for different branches of a family, or for different time periods.

Use standard genealogical abbreviations to list vital information (birth date, death date, married, unmarried, etc.). What follows is a short list of abbreviations.[1]

b.	born
bapt.	baptized
d.	died
d.unm.	died unmarried

---

[1] The list is adapted from David Hey, *The Oxford Guide to Family History* (Oxford: Oxford University Press, 1993), p. 159.

This gathering to welcome Japanese Emperor Hirohito to Newport News, Virginia, in 1975 gave Japanese Americans an opportunity to proudly express the two aspects of their identity. Researching Japanese American family history gives you the same opportunity.

d.s.p. died without children (in Latin, *decessit sine prole*)
dau. daughter
s. son
div. divorced
unm. unmarried
= married
I left descendants

As you continue your research, correcting mistakes and finding new information, it is a good idea to continue updating the family tree(s) as you go along. So do not be discouraged if early attempts look skimpy or disorganized. The more you revise and update a family tree, the more expert-looking it will become. You can also use computer software to create and maintain your family trees.

Preserving Your History

If you have organized the material in file folders as described in chapter 3, your job will be that much easier. The data you have gathered—documents, notes, charts, interview transcripts—will all be filed according to family groups or households. Photos will be mounted in photo albums, numbered and identified.

You can now take this material (except the photographs, which should remain in albums) and organize it into a book manuscript. Each family group section makes up a chapter. Mark the beginning of each chapter with dividers or a separate page with the chapter name written on it. Now you can bind it into a book. The easiest way is to use a three-ring binder. Three-ring binders are convenient for research because you can insert and remove pages easily. For permanent binding, however, they are less useful. Pages can fall out too easily for permanent storage.

Unless you are willing to have your family history bound into a hardcover book, your best bet may be velo binding with acetate covers. This is probably the sturdiest type of binding short of actual bookbinding and is relatively inexpensive. Most print shops and copy centers can bind your book while you wait. Spiral binding is another type of binding. As with three-ring binders, however, pages in a spiral-bound book tend to fall out.

If you are especially pleased with your family history, you might consider publishing it. There are companies known as subsidy publishers, or vanity presses, that will produce from your manuscript a finished book like this one and print multiple copies—several dozen or several hundred, however many you request. You will have to pay a fee for this service. There are also numerous guides on publishing for writers; the best known is *Writer's Market*, which is updated yearly.

There are numerous subsidy publishers throughout the country. Check the "Publishers" section in your local *Yellow Pages*. If you call a publishing company, the first thing to ask is whether or not they are a subsidy publisher or vanity press.

One thing you must do is make certain you have an accurate record of the source of each piece of information. For instance, interview transcripts should have the informant's name, date, place (see chapter 5); a photocopy of a document from the National Archives should be labeled "National Archives" along with the branch from which it came; pedigree charts should have your name (or whoever prepared it), along with home address and date; and any personal notes should have your name, approximate dates, and a brief descriptive title or heading at the top of each page (for example, "Kimitake, November 1995, Notes on Kawabata family, San Francisco"). This source information is invaluable to anyone who might want to follow your footsteps and continue the family history search you have started.

Writing Your Autobiography

If you are preparing your own family's history, you should include a chapter about yourself. This is a convenient way to introduce the book. Also, years from now one of your descendants may read your family history. He or she will be delighted to read your autobiography and treat it as a family

heirloom—along with the rest of the family history. Think
how much easier your search would have been if everyone
in the family had written a short autobiography. Write down
all the information you wish your ancestors had written
down.

Even if you have not researched your own family, you can
still write your autobiography. By setting down your experiences on paper, you may be surprised to discover how event-
ful and diverse your life has been thus far. Write about your
family, friends, neighbors, classmates, teachers. Describe
your home, your hometown, the people who live there. It is
not necessary to start with your birth and describe each day
after. Start with any memory that comes to mind—an event,
a place, a person.

The task of telling the story of your life sounds enormous
and a little intimidating. Some of what you remember might
be difficult, even painful to write about. Be as honest and
straightforward as you can. Try not to take yourself too
seriously. Once started, it becomes difficult to stop. One
memory leads to another. Before you know it, you have
story upon story; the world of your past comes to life.

Consider the example of the novelist Reynolds Price.
Asked to give a speech at a gathering, he decided to retell
stories from his college days. He describes the process of
gathering memories in preparation for his speech:

> The act of finding the history and setting it down filled an
> easy few days. And though I've always had a fair memory,
> this time I managed to surprise myself. I'd write down a
> fact—say, the location and dimensions of my freshman
> room in 1951—and the measured space would prove to
> be, not an isolated spot in my mind but the visible nub of
> a hidden string that, pulled on gently, unreeled itself as
> yards long, invariably branched and hung with more
> stored pictures than I'd known I possessed.
>
> Or better maybe, I'd make a list of hard facts—teachers,
> courses, the names of lost friends. And once set down on
> the page before me, they'd prove to be only the exposed

glints of abundant veins. Quickly I knew much more than I could use. . . .[2]

These memories eventually grew into his memoir of childhood, *Clear Pictures*.

Whether researching a family history or writing your own autobiography, your project is the same: the preservation of memory. The novelist Eudora Welty once said this about the power of memory:

The memory is a living thing . . . all that is remembered joins, and lives—the old and the young, the past and the present, the living and the dead.[3]

---

[2] Reynolds Price, *Clear Pictures* (New York: Atheneum, 1989), p. 6.

[3] Eudora Welty, *One Writer's Beginnings* (Cambridge: Harvard University Press, 1984), p. 104.

Resources

FAMILY TREES

Hey, David. *The Oxford Guide to Family History.*
Oxford, U.K.: Oxford University Press, 1993.

Though written for people living in England, it provides useful general information on creating a family tree. Bibliography, illustrations, index.

JAPANESE MEMOIRS

Dazai, Osamu. *Return to Tsugaru: Reminiscences.*
Translated from the Japanese by James Westerhoven.
New York: Kodansha, 1985.

A famous Japanese novelist takes a trip back to the countryside of his birthplace to retrace his own past.

Kurosawa, Akira. *Something Like an Autobiography.*
New York: Vintage, 1984.

One of the world's most famous movie directors gives an account of his life and career; of special interest are the early chapters, which describe his growing up in Japan in the years between the two world wars.

JAPANESE AMERICAN MEMOIRS

Houston, Jeanne Wakatsuki, and Houston, James D.
Farewell to Manzanaar. New York: Bantam Books, 1979.

A woman's recollection of growing up during World War

II, and her struggle to reconcile her twin inheritance of Japanese and American cultures.

Masumoto, David Mas. *Epitaph for a Peach: Four Seasons on My Family Farm*. San Francisco: Harper San Francisco, 1995.

For three generations the Masumoto family owned a peach and grape farm in California. This memoir tells of their experiences and the author's own efforts to save the family's farm and its traditions from industrialization.

Minatoya, Lydia. *Talking to High Monks in the Snow: An Asian American Odyssey*. New York: HarperCollins, 1992.

The memoir of a Japanese American woman who travels to Japan, where she meets her mother's family for the first time and learns more about her Japanese legacy.

Mura, David. *Turning Japanese: Memoirs of a Sansei*. New York: Atlantic Monthly Press, 1991.

The memoir of a third-generation Japanese American from Chicago who spent a year in Japan. It is at once the story of a person tracing his roots and a portrait of contemporary Japan.

Okimoto, Daniel. *American in Disguise*. New York: Weatherhill, 1977.

By a second-generation Japanese American, this is the story of his family's experience in the United States, from his parents' arrival in the 1930s to their internment in World War II to his journey as an adult to Japan for the first time. It gives a portrait of Japanese Americans and their place in American society.

Sone, Monica. *Nisei Daughter*. Seattle: University of Washington Press, 1979.

A woman's personal account of her early childhood in

Seattle during the 1930s and her experiences during the relocation of Japanese Americans during World War II.

Uchida, Yoshiko. *Desert Exile: The Uprooting of a Japanese American Family.* **Seattle: University of Washington Press, 1984.**

The story of one family's experiences amid the turmoil of the Japanese American internment during World War II.

GUIDES TO WRITING AND PUBLISHING

Achtert, Walter S., and Gibaldi, Joseph. *The MLA Style Manual.* **New York: Modern Language Association, 1985.**

Guide for writers, with tips on grammar, diction, syntax, etc. The standard style for college composition classes.

Bove, Tony. *The Art of Desktop Publishing.* **New York: Bantam Books, 1990.**

A guide to creating professional-looking documents with a desktop program with pagemaking and graphic applications.

The Chicago Manual of Style: The Essential Guide for Writers, Editors, and Publishers, **14th Ed. Chicago: University of Chicago Press, 1993.**

The standard guide to correct grammar, syntax, and style used by most publishers in the United States.

Gouldrup, Lawrence. *Writing the Family Narrative.* **Salt Lake City: Ancestry Inc., 1987.**

A beginner's guide to writing a family history, with tips on the fundamentals of prose narrative and examples.

Lackey, Richard. *Cite Your Sources: A Manual for Documenting Family Histories and Genealogical*

Records. Jackson: University Press of Mississippi, 1980.

A guide to proper citation of sources, everything from documents to gravestones.

———. *Write It Right: A Manual for Writing Family Histories and Genealogies.* Falmouth, VA: Board for Certification of Genealogists, 1981.

A rare but valuable guide for beginners to writing a family history.

Strunk, William, and White, E. B. *The Elements of Style*, rev. ed. New York: Macmillan, 1979.

The classic style reference guide, usually referred to as "Strunk and White." It is still required reading in many college composition classes.

Zinsser, William. *On Writing Well: An Informed Guide to Writing Nonfiction.* New York: Harper & Row, 1985.

A step-by-step manual for writing prose, from organization to the last draft.

SUBSIDY PUBLISHERS

Carlton Press
11 West 32nd Street
Dept. NYE
New York, NY 10011
212-714-0300

The guide *How to Publish Your Book* can be ordered by mail or telephone.

New Century Publishers
410 Massachusetts Avenue
Norfolk, VA 23508
804-627-0853

Morris Publishing
3212 East Highway 30
Kearney, NE 68847
800-650-7888, extension NYR6

Vantage Press
516 West 34th Street
New York, NY 10001
800-821-3990

Write or call for a free guidebook to self-publishing. Ask
for brochure TD-2.

Glossary

ane   Older sister.

anecdote   Brief story about an interesting incident.

ani   Older brother.

artifact   Object, such as a tool, produced by human workmanship.

buranke katsugi   Blanket carriers; *issei* farm workers who moved from farm to farm.

chichi   Familiar form of "father" (used only when talking about one's own father).

chōjō   Eldest daughter.

chonan   Eldest son.

customs   Taxes on imports.

dekaseginin   Temporary emigrant workers.

dekasegi shosei   Student laborers.

diaspora   Scattering of a people with a common origin.

emissary   Person or agent sent on a specific mission.

evacuee   Person who has been removed from a location.

gaman   Attitude of trying to make the best of a bad situation without complaint.

gannenmono   "First-year men" on Hawaiian plantations; the first 150 Japanese laborers recruited from Yokohama and brought to Hawaii.

generation   Group of people who make up a single step in the line of descent from an ancestor.

go-ryōshin   Someone else's parents.

haha   Familiar form of "mother" (used only when talking about one's own mother).

ihai   Mortuary tablet that stands on a family altar and is inscribed with information about a person's life.

imōto   Younger sister.

imōto-san   Respectful form of "younger sister" (never used when speaking to one's younger sister).

internment   Confinement during a war.

issei   Japanese who immigrated to the United States.

joseki   Records of persons who have died or married and been removed from *koseki*.

kakocho   Buddhist death register.

keigo   Levels of politeness.

keizu   Professionally prepared genealogy of aristocratic families.

koseki   Family register of members.

kugakusei   Student.

kuroshio   Black Current; the rough seas that sometimes swept Japanese fishing boats to the Hawaiian islands.

musuko   Son.

musume   Daughter.

narrative   Story.

naturalization   To receive the rights of a citizen.

nisei   Children of the *issei*, born in the United States.

nuptial   Of or relating to marriage or a wedding.

oba   Aunt.

obā   Grandmother.

oba-san   Respectful form of "aunt."

obā-san   Respectful form of "grandmother."

oji   Uncle.

ojii   Grandfather.

ojii-san   Respectful form of "grandfather."

oji-san   Respectful form of "uncle."

okā-san   Respectful form of "mother."

onee-san   Respectful form of "older sister."

onii-san   Respectful form of "older brother."

otō-san   Respectful form of "father."

otōto   Younger brother.

otōto-san   Respectful form of "younger brother" (never used when speaking to one's younger brother).

parliamentary   Related to a country's supreme legislative body.

pedigree   An ancestral line.

recollection   Something that is remembered.

relic   Souvenir or memento.

reparations   Money paid in compensation for wrongs committed by a nation.

ryōshin   One's own parents.

Sannen ganbatte kaeru   Work hard for three years and then return home.

sansei   Children of the *nisei*.

shashin kekkon   Picture bride marriage.

Shikata ga nai   It can't be helped.

warlord   Military commander who also exercises power by force over civilians.

Index

ABOUT THE AUTHOR
Yoji Yamaguchi was born in Kearny, New Jersey in 1963. He is the author of *Face of a Stranger*, a novel. He currently lives in New York City, where he works in the publishing industry.

ILLUSTRATION CREDITS
Cover: © Larry Dale Gordon/The Image Bank; cover inset and pp. 3, 19, 21, 23, 26, 30, 32, 34, 37, 39, 41, 42, 47, 50, 51, 83, 86, 99, 109, 127, 130, 142, 153, BETTMAN. Color insert: pp. 2, 3, 4, 5, 6, 8, 9, 10, 11, 16, BETTMAN; p. 7, © Rick, Gerharter/Impact Visuals; p. 12, © Clark Jones/Impact Visuals; p. 13, © Mark Ludak/Impact Visuals; p. 14, © Larry Dale Gordon/The Image Bank; p. 15, © Rick Reinhard/Impact Visuals.

LAYOUT AND DESIGN
Kim Sonsky